THE
MAKING
OF A
DRUID

THE
MAKING
OF A
DRUID

Hidden Teachings
from
The Colloquy of Two Sages

CHRISTIAN-J. GUYONVARC'H

Translated by
CLARE MARIE FROCK

Inner Traditions
Rochester, Vermont

Inner Traditions International
One Park Street
Rochester, Vermont 05767
www.InnerTraditions.com

First U.S. edition published by Inner Traditions in 2002

Originally published in French under the title *Le Dialogue des deux sages* by Éditions Payot & Rivages

LIBRARY OF CONGRESS CATALOGING-IN-PUBLICATION DATA

Guyonvarc'h, Christian J.
[Dialogue des deux sages. English]
The making of a druid : hidden teachings from the colloquy
of two sages / Christian J. Guyonvarc'h ;
translated by Clare Marie Frock.—1st U.S. ed.
p. cm.
ISBN 0-89281-874-3
1. Imcallam in da thuarad. 2. Druids and Druidism.
I. Imcallam in da thuarad. English. II. Title.

BL910 .I53 G8913 2002
299'.16—dc21   2001051515

Printed and bound in Canada

10   9   8   7   6   5   4   3   2   1

Text design and layout by Virginia L. Scott Bowman
This book was typeset in Goudy with Goudy Lombardic Caps
as the display typeface

Contents

Preface

IN THE VAST SPHERE of insular Celtic literature, particularly of that in Gaelic, the reader (or scholar) and lover of Irish (or at times, but much less frequently, Welsh) texts is rarely confronted with problems other than the literary ones concerning epic narrative and mythology. With the legal texts being difficult of access and with the poetry being even less accessible, owing to its technical complexity, what remain are didactic texts, and, risking boredom, the ecclesiastical texts and the annals with their cumbersome critical apparatus. All of these are far from being interesting to the same degree, and it is obvious—paradoxically enough—that a large part of the texts written in neo-Celtic languages—Irish, Welsh or Breton—would be incapable of holding the undivided attention of an inexperienced reader.

It would be easy here to draw disillusioned conclusions about the absence of metaphysical texts, that is, texts that could be called discursive commentaries on religious concepts, or what is presently called, generally and imprecisely, "spirituality." If we were to judge from their literature, the Gaels, like the rest of the Celts, are little gifted in philosophical abstractions and discussions, the teaching and training in which being the mark left by the Greeks and the

Romans on the Europeans. But this is a late assertion, made about a language whose elites more or less abandoned its usage starting in the seventeenth century, and, what is more, they did not transmit everything to us. Neither in Welsh nor in Breton is there philosophy—and for even more serious reasons. In the Middle Ages, when all people serious about Christianity spoke only the common and international language of Latin among themselves, the Irish, and even the Breton clerks studying at the Sorbonne, did not make such a bad impression. But their native languages gained nothing from these intellectual exercises, with the exception of the borrowing of some Latin words. Earlier in history, the Irish were always appreciated in the court of Charlemagne; they were very knowledgeable and did not cost a lot! But it has always been more prudent to know Irish well in order to understand Hisperic Latin, that is, the form of Latin written in Ireland in the High Middle Ages. And closer to our times, the Breton *Catholicon*, a trilingual dictionary in Breton, Latin, and French—which is also the first French dictionary, dating back to 1464—was made for the "poor clerks from Brittany" who, knowing French very poorly as it was, misused Latin outrageously. The author wanted to keep them from putting *squamas avibus et plumas piscibus*, "scales on birds and feathers on fish," that is, from committing gross errors in the elementary use of Latin.[1]

All this is to say how, in all the Celtic countries, at least as long as they are Celtophone, there is always the obstacle of language and, in a good many cases, this obstacle is

---

[1]See the introduction by the author in the reproduction of the Jehan Calvez edition (Tréguier, 1499), in *Celticum* 22 (Rennes, 1975), pp. xxvii–xxviii.

definitive because the manner of expression differs so much from that of Romance and Germanic languages. Total comprehension of certain dialectical Breton or Irish texts is still a difficult exercise for a non-Celtophone (consider, to give just one example, the five allomorphs of the verb "to be" in Breton!). It was d'Arbois de Jubainville, the famous and well-respected Celticist, who wondered how to translate the little Irish sentence, *nifhiulim-sa mór leis* (now we would write *nilim-sa*), literally, "I am not great with him," which should be understood as "I am not on good terms with him," or "He does not think highly of me."

It is the thousands of possible examples of this kind in one or another of the Celtic languages currently still spoken that come to mind as I introduce this translation of *The Colloquy of Two Sages*. For, however exceptional or unusual this may seem, at issue here is a truly unique text, a dialogue between two druids concerning the knowledge required of a candidate aspiring to the grade of doctor that also contains the customs of language and expression of the Celtic priestly class. To say that the knowledge, the language, and even the vocabulary, peppered with metaphors—sometimes on two or three levels—are at first glance difficult for us to understand is still saying very little. Immediate, literal understanding is sometimes a futile exercise that does not allow one to reach complete, symbolic, and deep understanding of a text. Yet, normally, one does not go without the other.

Perhaps this explains why, in over a century, very few Celtic scholars have given their attention to the *Colluquy*, and, even if they have understood its primary or superficial meaning, they have sought no further because for them the limit of possible explanations was immediately reached. The science of the two druids of the *Colluquy* was no longer taken seriously, for reasons that it would be better not to go into too much, but that clearly come from what could be called scholarly dryness. And yet the Irish themselves went to the trouble, many times, of copying and recopying a text whose clarity is not its best quality but whose content represented or condensed a whole part of their culture. That more than a dozen copies exist, in various manuscripts dating from between the twelfth and nineteenth centuries, is undeniable proof of interest. It is true that what interested the people of centuries past is no longer always what interests our contemporaries. It is true as well that medieval Irish, for various reasons, is not a language widely taught in Western universities, lagging far behind Sanskrit! But this is, at least in the present case, because no one knew how to read it very well. I hope that I have, at least this once in my modest career as a Celticist, filled a gap in the availability of the traditional texts of old Europe and in so doing, put to right the grave injustice of oblivion.

Introduction

The Subject of the
Colloquy of Two Sages

There is some question whether different copies of the *Colloquy of Two Sages* are referred to in the catalog of d'Arbois de Jubainville.[1] In d'Arbois this text is called *Agallam in dá Suad*, and the title is translated as "Dialogue of the Two Doctors," which is different from the title Whitley Stokes used in 1905 in the *Revue Celtique*, *Immacallam in dá Thúarad*, "The Colloquy of the Two Sages." The translation is different as well, though d'Arbois's is not very exact; for example, *suí* means "sage" and not "doctor" (which would be *ollam*). It could just as well be said, not incorrectly, that this is a "dialogue of two druids."[2] But we shall disregard here contingencies of philology. The interested reader may find details about the manuscripts and textual references in the notes.

The text is placed by d'Arbois in the cycle of Conchobar and Cúchulainn, in other words in the epic Ulster Cycle, but we do not know why he would have placed in

---

[1]*Essai d'un catalogue de la littérature épique de l'Irlande* (Paris, 1883), pp. 5–6.
[2]See the end of note 2, p. 71.

that epic a narrative of what must have been, from the outset, a pedagogical and initiatory text making up part of the general knowledge of any scholar. The sole pretext for this dating could only be the fact that the dialogue takes place at Emain Macha, capital of Ulster, with the intervention of the mythical character Bricriu, and there are references to King Conchobar, King Ailill, and Queen Medb as well. But this intrusion of extrinsic characters has value only as an exterior reference point; it has absolutely no real historical value. It simply constitutes a way to connect the *Colloquy* to the myths gathered within the Ulster Cycle, where the mere presence of Bricriu suffices to provoke a misunderstanding in the form of a quarrel. This, however, has no significant bearing on the content itself of the *Colloquy*.

The Colloquy of Two Sages is, in effect, nothing like an ordinary narrative account; nor is it anything like an epic in any way whatsoever; rather, it could be related, with some reservations, to the quite specialized genre of both prophecy and *tecosca*, or didactic and pedagogical teachings. In fact, this is not a teaching intended for a student, and it is not classifiable for the reason that has already been stated, namely, it is unique as a work of druidic teaching, and this is where its primary significance lies. No other known Irish text is comparable to it. The only other text that bears any resemblance to it, the *Acallamh ná Senórach*, or "Colloquy of the Elders," is primarily epic rather than didactic. Its main purpose is to have Cailte, an old companion of Finn, tell Saint Patrick, newly come to Ireland, of the Fianna's adventures throughout the land.[3]

---

[3]Standish O'Grady, *Silva Gadelica* (London, 1892), vol. 1, pp. 94–233, and Whitley Stokes, *Irische Texte* (Leipzig, 1900), vol. 4, pp. ix–xiv and 1–224, 225–435.

I will say that our *Colloquy* is archaic mainly by its content, perhaps more so than by its language, which is, *grosso modo*, Middle Irish, most likely prior to the twelfth century, which is the transcription date of the *Book of Leinster*. It must be understood as well that the content of the text is infinitely older than the transcription and than the language itself.

The Whitley Stokes Edition

The most common edition of the *Colloquy* has been the Whitley Stokes edition of 1892. This edition was the basis for the fragments I translated in *Les Druides* in 1986. I consulted it again for the present work, but I reviewed and frequently modified my original translation, and for the part of the text confirmed by the *Book of Leinster,* I verified, and when needed, replaced Whitley Stokes's interpretations with those of the diplomatic edition, henceforth indispensable.[4] There are a few differences of interpretation, of little significance with regard to meaning, but in the event of divergence, the reading of the diplomatic edition must be favored. I followed this same edition systematically for the line breaks and glosses.

Whitley Stokes's work includes, as do almost all of the Irish translations by this scholar, a brief introduction, the Irish text with an English translation on the facing page, and a glossary of the most important words at the end. Footnotes explain or comment upon the principal lexical or grammatical difficulties.

[4]R. I. Best and M. A. O'Brien, eds., *The Book of Leinster, formerly Lebar ná Núachongbála* (Dublin, 1965), vol. 4, pp. 815–32, folios 186a.12 to 188c.60, lines 24196–855.

This way of working generally suffices for those texts that present no special difficulties. Over the course of his long career as a Celticist, Whitley Stokes has in this way done us the great service of making several dozen Irish narratives immediately accessible, and in unquestionably reliable versions.[5]

Although an excellent philologist, Whitley Stokes was less gifted in religious exegesis. In his edition of the *Colloquy*, the notes are much too brief, and his work is much too scanty for a text of this importance. The problem is that since the beginning of the century, Celtic religious studies have changed somewhat. In his summary of the *Colloquy*, in effect, Stokes sees in it no more than a game of question and answer between a young optimistic poet, or *file*, and an old pessimistic *file*, each following his personal inclination. One describes the events of a favorable future; the other resolves to enumerate a whole succession of coming or imminent disasters, natural or otherwise. In fact, the *Colloquy* is not this at all. Or rather, it is something else altogether.

Neither does Whitley Stokes correct the error committed by d'Arbois de Jubainville in his *Cours de littérature celtique* when he supposes that Ireland experienced division and rivalry between the druids and the *filid* who formed into rival guilds.[6] After this, it was believed that Christianization happened to the advantage of the *filid* and at the expense of the druids, and this error hindered research for a very long time.[7] This error still persists sporadically in the works of some authors.

---

[5] The *Colloquy* appeared in several collections, chief among them the *Zeitschrift für Celtische Philologie*, the *Revue Celtique*, and the *Irische Texte* by Windisch.

[6] *Les Celtes et les langues celtiques*, p. 129 ff.

[7] Corrected in Françoise Le Roux and Christian-J. Guyonvarc'h, *Les Druides*, (Rennes: Ouest-France, 1986), p. 45 ff., as well as the error concerning the bards' inferior rank in Ireland.

Whitley Stokes did not understand that the game of subtly doled-out questions and answers does not depend upon the actual will of the two participants in the dialogue. Rather, the give-and-take conforms to the use of certain questions within well-determined circumstances and follows specific rules and criteria, most of which escape us but which are very definitely the consequence of a structured and organized teaching, with such and such a question obligatorily calling for such and such a response, all with a very narrow margin for freedom. In the medieval Irish concept of teaching, an ignorant person, or someone whose training is incomplete, is normally reduced to silence with such questions. This already resembles somewhat the scholastic rigor of the medieval university. From the first reading, the *Colloquy*, like many of the texts of the ancient traditions—especially the Eastern ones—seems dull, and even lifeless or insipid; it must be reread two or three times to absorb truly all the richness it contains or implies and, finally, to discern that which gives it its substance.

It can be affirmed straightaway that the *Colloquy* is at times more interesting by what it allows to be glimpsed, construed, specified, or implied than by what it says clearly or directly. Through the little that it has salvaged, the Christianization of Ireland makes us regret even more keenly all that we have lost. But the posthumous case of Gaul would deserve a hundredfold the lamentations of the Celticists.

Something else is bothersome in the Whitley Stokes edition: the text of the *Colloquy* is divided into a large number of very short paragraphs, often of a single line, whose content is almost always taken up again by a gloss that clarifies or paraphrases it, and more rarely, comments on or explains it. In the edition published in the *Revue Celtique*, only a very small part of these glosses has been translated. This is a gap that must be filled, at least in the majority of cases, because it happens fairly often that the gloss provides an explanatory component not included in the body of the text. And furthermore, these glosses are old enough that they should be an integral part (and should have been for a long time now) of the primary material of the *Colloquy*.

Presentation of the Text

Because the glosses in the text are so numerous, and, as many of them are merely simple repetitions or paraphrases that add nothing to the meaning and this edition is not being devoted to pure philology, our problem is resolved by including only those glosses that offer any significance for the interpretation and elucidation of the text. It would be pointless to overload this translation with dozens of paraphrases or reiterations that do nothing to further its understanding or its interest. There are already too many philologically inclined notes that are crucial to the explication of this exceptional *Colloquy*. The reader will have to bear with the occasional citation in the notes of an Irish word whose particular meaning calls for an explanation or a justification to help in the general understanding of the whole.

The existence of such a large quanity of glosses when compared to the size of the raw text is, moreover, a remarkable fact and a piece of evidence that helps us understand the genesis of the *Colloquy*. Until now, no one seems to have seen or understood that this unique text is our principal means—if not our first opportunity—for understanding a pre-Christian, Celtic pedagogy, the very same one that Caesar talked about in the brief paragraph devoted to the druids, in his *De bello gallico* (6.13). As the *Colloquy* shows, an identical pedagogy existed in Ireland, and in fact it is far more complex than Whitley Stokes had supposed.

At the outset, it is necessary to think of the text as an oral joust in a difficult and complicated language, the one reserved for the *filid* and the druids, the *berla filid*, or "language of the poets," which is sometimes still called *berla Fené*, or "language of the *Féné*"—Féné being another name for the Irish. The line between this "language of the poets" and the common language was very probably the same as that which separated common language from that of the gods, that is, all the words and turns of phrase that were used to speak to the gods and, eventually, the language in which the gods expressed themselves in order to speak to men.[8] In other words, the question here concerns distant survival of the *sacred* language common to all the Celtic druids;[9] more prosaically, the language of the Irish priestly class in its "poetic" and literary (in the contemporary sense of the term) aspect has been studied often.[10]

We can thank the narrative called *Echtra Cormaic i Tir Tairngiri ocus Ceart Claidib Cormaic*, or "The Adventures of Cormac in the Land of Promise and the Law of Cormac's Sword," from both the *Book of Ballymote* and the *Yellow Book of Lecan*, for an introduction to the tradition of Irish "ordeals," and an authorized indigenous opinion on what had perhaps become the language of a class more than the language of the gods:

---

[8]With regard to the Greek field, cf. Françoise Bader's study, "La langue des dieux: hermétisme et autobiographie," *Études classiques* 58, no. 1 (Namur, 1990), pp. 2–26.

[9]See p. 74, n. 8.

[10]One will find more on this subject in Morton W. Bloomfield and Charles W. Dunn, *The Role of the Poet in Early Societies* (Cambridge, 1989).

The nobles of the men of Ireland said that every man should be treated according to what was due him, whether kings or doctors, the insane, tenant farmers or soldiers, and all [social] classes as well. For they were sure that the arrangements made in Ireland at the assembly of the men of Fodla would be that they would stay there forever. For since the time when the poet Amairgen of the White Knee had given his first judgment in Ireland, until the colloquy, in Emain Macha, of the two sages, namely, Ferchertne the poet and Nede, son of Adna, concerning the robe of the highest-placed doctor, only the poets had the right of judgment. Obscure is how the words that these poets said seemed to everyone in this discussion, and the legal decision that they delivered was not clear for the kings and the other poets. "These men alone," said the kings, "have their judgment, their art and their knowledge. First and foremost, we do not understand what they say." "Indeed," said Conchobar, "starting from today. But the judgment which is their own, this aside, will not pass. Everyone will take part." And in this way the poets were deprived of their judicial power, except for what was their own. And each man of Ireland took part in the law.[11]

It is inconceivable that the men of the Middle Ages understood nothing of all this. They certainly understood the words, with very few exceptions. It was the connection between the ideas and their symbolic significance that escaped them. And the poets were asked to speak like everyone, which was very obviously unbefitting to ask of the Irish *filid*.

---

[11]*Irische Texte*, vol. 3, pp. 186–87.

From the start, therefore, we must think of a hermetic text learned by heart by the candidate-*filid* or candidate-druids, and becoming more and more comprehensible to them as the master explained and commented upon its terms. There remains a trace of this mode of teaching in the glosses. Then, at the time of transcription, all this had to be simplified or partially cut, and, not all of it being perfectly understood, the whole was transformed into a more accessible language, phrase by phrase and almost word by word, with all the errors, gibberish, "repairs"—and, above all, omissions—inherent in the transition from oral to written. Add to this the fact of Christian censorship following the conversion of Ireland and we have the explanation for the occasionally imperfect condition of the handwritten versions that have come down to us. The original *Colloquy* must have been quite different from what we now have in front of us, and, it certainly must have been more complete.

It is possible, however, to draw a comparison between the systematic manner in which certain monks reading the Holy Scriptures in the Vulgate wrote the glosses to the Epistles of Paul. The gloss, at least in this respect, is certainly the written equivalent or consequence of a very old Celtic practice of "commenting" on a basic "text."

Christianization was in all likelihood the sole cause of the expurgation of the *Colloquy*; it is clear that most subjects or words contrary to the principles of Christian faith were deleted or toned down and that the text was "redressed" in small ways in more Christian garb. This explains the references to a few clerical formulae as well as the reference, which also became common—all the way into the epic texts of the same sort as *The Cattle Raid of Cooley*—to the Last Judgment.

We can be sure that the text lost some of its original

flavor in being thus watered down, and it did not thereby become any more accessible; it was the glosses that then became the trickiest part to elucidate, if not to translate. Some are close to incoherent. The wording of a few others proves that much was no longer understood by the last transcribers, or else that scribal tradition had been muddled for a very long time. In any case, all the philological and linguistic knowledge of our times is powerless to discern or restore the first traditional version. We must be content with the fragments that have survived and that—sometimes—we guess at more than see clearly.

In general, the *filid* of Ireland had a very high opinion of themselves, of their titles, and of their science, and almost the whole of the *Colloquy* bears witness to this fact. Only one place suited them, justified by their knowledge, and this was the first; they determined—rightly so, undoubtedly—that their fees had to be handsome, without comparison to the modest salaries of the academics of what is now called Western Europe. Thus they join the Brahmans of India, and I believe, the representatives of all the authentic priesthoods. Neither is there any pride in this *Colloquy*, in the Christian sense of pride as a "mortal sin"; this is, very simply, merely the attitude of people conscious of what they are and of what they represent. In one sense, within the context—at times indefinable in human terms—of the primordial tradition, one could compare *The Colloquy of Two Sages*, making all due allowances and reservations, to the *I Ching*, that divinatory treatise consisting of maxims, each followed by a commentary and an explanation. And I would apply to the Celtic druids the following formula from the *I Ching*, magnificent in its lucid concision: "The sage distances himself from vulgar people, not out of hate but out of dignity."[12]

The Significance of the Text

The main significance of *The Colloquy of Two Sages*, which, as already stated, could very well have been entitled "Dialogue of Two Druids" without changing a single word of the text, is that it is not what we find exclusively in the Irish repertoire, namely epic or mythological narratives containing no indication of a higher order like that found in the Brāhmaṇas, the Vedas, or the Upaniṣads of Indian "literature," or in the tedious pseudohistorical annals.

In fact, whereas Sanskrit scholars may suffer more from an overabundance of texts, Celticists often see themselves as condemned, by the quantitative scarcity of their sources, to comparisons or to deductions, often condensed or risky. In any case, nothing allows for the leisure of reaching or brushing against the metaphysical summits of the commentaries or teachings of which India is so prodigal. Moreover, it would never have occurred to the mind of a single European or American Celticist of the first half of the twentieth century that this terrain had ever existed or that any trace of it, however tenuous, would ever be discovered. The Celtic religion was thought to have issued from barbarians given to human sacrifice, incapable of the slightest intellectual performance, and whose only intelligence had been to convert, rather late, to Roman ways and culture.

The *Colloquy* is, in this regard, a happy exception. Not that it singlehandedly fills all the doctrinal gaps in the

---

[12]*Yi King, le livre des mutations*, translated and annotated by Raymond de Becker (Paris: Planète, 1970), p. 180. Translation from the French by Clare Frock.

narrative or didactic accounts, but in that it is our only text of this type, and it provides enough clues or leads, despite the formal Christianization that characterizes it, to give us a few accurate views of some ancient Celtic concepts. Let us say that it confirms more often than it informs. Obviously, this fact does not replace what we would have hoped to find because, all things considered, if the *Colloquy*, from the traditional point of view, remains fairly scanty—at least we are not totally deprived.

The *Colloquy* is also and above all a form of thought and expression to which Western mentalities have become alien. This is a result, in part, of the archaic language and the linguistic structures, which are unusual for anyone who speaks and writes one or the other of the great European languages, and which includes the verb phrase being always at the beginning of a clause; the absence of relative pronouns and verbal expressions of relation; the systematic and syntactical use of the facts of *samdhi*, or consonantal and syntactic changes; the predominance of nominal expression over verbal expression; the degeneration of the primitive Indo-European word system; and the innumerable internal complications arising from the continual creation of substitute forms. Things have have been taken to a point where a few linguists, and not the least among them, have believed for a long time that the Celtic verb, far from being Indo-European, could be of Hamitic or substratal origin.[13] Still, everything that we know about the druids and the *filid*, or the bards and the seers, in Gaul as well as in Ireland, indirectly—but absolutely—contradicts this hypothesis.

---

[13]The reader may refer to what I have said about this in the introduction to *The Cattle Raid of Cooley* (Paris: Gallimard, 1994), pp. 25–26.

The Consequences of Christianization

Added to all that has been discussed so far are the consequences, immediate or remote, of the Christianization of
the Celtic countries, and of Ireland in particular. It is not
heresy to say that, in practical terms, starting from the
fifth century A.D., the insular Celts lost their cultural
autonomy when they stopped having a Celtophone elite
transmitting a totally independent culture. The impact of
Christianity was enormous and definitive with the conversion, without a doubt massive, of the pre-Christian
priestly class (druids and *filid*) and the adoption of Latin
as the common liturgical language and the language of
culture. Post-patrician Ireland of the High Middle Ages
thus became bilingual before becoming trilingual with the
Scandinavian invasions, then quadrilingual with the Nor-
man barons and the English conquest. It is sometimes difficult to delimit the reciprocal influences throughout
history of Gaelic, Latin, Old Norse, French, and English
(I resist the idea, which has occurred to a few scholars, of
considering Old Norse one of Ireland's languages of culture!). But Latin, implanted first, was predominant. It did
not become the common language as it did in Gaul; however, it did give rise to some very serious disturbances in
the lexicon. All the religious and intellectual vocabulary
was transformed or replaced by Latin borrowings, and it
took on all the Christian liturgical vocabulary, which
arrived via the intermediary of the British languages. It is
almost a miracle that the pre-Christian word for "sacrifice"—Old Irish *idpart*, Modern Irish *iobairt*—was preserved to mean "the Eucharist," or that the adjective
naomh, "holy," which etymologically means "vigor," was
not replaced as in British (Welsh and Breton *sani*) by a

borrowing of the Latin *sanctus*. All, or almost all, was disturbed.[14]

With this disruption, the understanding of the sacred was made very difficult, if not impossible. Without the example and the helpful comparison of the Indian tradition, used on other occasions (for example, regarding the sea-urchin fossil[15]), I would never have had the ambition nor even the intention to persevere. But let's not kindle any illusions: even if we can from time to time sniff out traces of it, Celtic esotericism is no longer directly accessible to us. Equally far from the innumerable Celtomanic platitudes and from the dry as dust proclivities of academia, the merit of this too brief *Colloquy*—with its seemingly simplistic and even naive expression—is to have us clearly understand that long ago an esotericism did once truly exist, but that it does not correspond in any way to the reveries of certain exegetes.

What saved Irish Celticness from total disappearance or breakdown is that Christianization was not accompanied or preceded by a Romanization comparable to that of Gaul or, to a lesser degree, to that of insular Brittany. Until the Scandinavian invasions of the eighth century, the political and social structures remained intact. These included the vertical hierarchy of the royalty, arranged by levels of kings of cantons and provinces, then by the supreme royalty of Tara; an exclusive rural habitat (Irish, like all the other neo-Celtic languages, has no indigenous word for "city"); the absence of any religious infrastructure comparable to that of the continental dioceses (the abbot of the

---

[14]Cf. my brief outline in the conclusion of *Magie, médecine et divination chez les Celtes* (Paris: Payot, 1997), pp. 352–54.

[15]See Le Roux and Guyonvarc'h, *Les Druides*, pp. 329–31.

monastery is at the same time the bishop); and, most importantly, the maintenance of ancestral rights and immense compendia of jurisprudence, put at a late date into writing and redone according to Christian norms, but which owe nothing to Roman law and which continued to be in use, despite the English presence, until the eighteenth century.

Nevertheless, Celtic Christianity, solidly and definitively established starting from the fifth century, and exclusively monastic and hermetic, sometimes seemed so strange to those on the Continent that it was looked upon as heretical or as the sequel to paganism; and the Vatican, distrustful of it, persisted relentlessly for several centuries in trying to erase all traces of it. Somewhat curiously, it was the Abbot of Landévennec in Brittany who was the last to submit, in 818. In Ireland, everything had been finished from the beginning of the seventh century.

The Originality of Irish Culture

The originality of Irish culture is that Celtic Christianity accepted or consecrated an Irish duality, the double legitimacy of a pre-Christian Ireland governed by oral or "natural" law (*recht aicnid*, or "law of nature") and a Christianized Ireland governed by conformity to the Holy Scriptures (*recht litre*, or "law of the letter"). There is no contradiction but rather juxtaposition, indeed symbiosis, of the two systems, between which the medieval Irish never saw any contradiction at all.

Tied to the "law of nature" was all of what the monk-transcribers, or Christianized *filid*, called the "history" of Ireland, and which was only, to a large extent, disguised or adapted mythology in the first stages of its slow degradation into folklore. Tied to the "law of the letter" was the immense body of ecclesiastical Irish literature; it started as early as 636 with a homily (preserved at the municipal library of Cambrai), then with glosses dispersed in the eighth and ninth centuries in almost all of Western and Central Europe, and has continued almost up to our era with a considerable body of literature.

And even though all of this is written, even though the Irish scholars became, until far into the nineteenth century, determined copyists, all Irish literature, whether epic, mythological, didactic, annalistic, or hagiographic, has retained an undeniable oral feel.

This is clearly because no Celtic language is capable, as is Latin or Greek, of rendering the long, complex sentences of barristers and lawyers or even philosophers and theologians. The Celtic sentence, with its verbs at the beginning of the phrase and its lack of relative pronouns, makes for rather lively and rapid, violent and colorful expression. It can certainly express everything, but not in the same manner as Latin or Greek. It adapts itself with much difficulty to philosophy, and the conversion to Christianity did not enrich it—much to the contrary—because the great minds like Scotus Erigena or Dichuil thought in Latin. Medieval Ireland did not fall to the lamentable level of ecclesiastical Breton such as one reads in the sixteenth-century texts, and especially those of the following centuries, but it gained no advantage because, helped by the decline of the nobility caused by the English persecution, Modern Irish ceased to be a language of universal culture.

Farther back in antiquity, the druids already had a reputation for speaking in enigmas. The Greeks were determined, for lack of a better word, to treat them as "philosophers," but they all note that their way of teaching their doctrines has nothing to do with the exceeding clarity of Greek thought: "Those who think that philosophy is an invention of the barbarians explain the systems in effect in each people. They say that the gymnosophists and the druids make their predictions through the means of enigmas and obscure phrases, teaching that one must worship the gods, not do harm, and keep a virile attitude."[16] Three centuries previous, Diodorus Siculus noted: "In conversation, their words are brief, enigmatic, proceeding from allusions and implications, often hyperbolic, where self-aggrandizement or minimization of others are concerned."[17] One could also quote those fifteenth-century Welsh poets who hoped to be understood only among themselves and only by a few people.[18] This is seen, or sensed; nothing had changed in the Middle Ages with regard to the essentials and the manner of expression. Furthermore, it could also be shown that, well into the twentieth century, popular Breton, which no longer has much more than the simple man's naive beliefs as its philosophy and its book-fodder, still teems with complicated and obscure maxims and riddles.

It can be seen, moreover, on actual evidence, that Irish Christianity, as it appears in the *Colloquy*, with a few inevitable formulaic insertions from the era of transcription, goes no further than the usual formalism of all the Celtic Christendoms, and in this case is scarcely more than a glossing over, as superficial as it is cumbersome. Though

---

[16]Diogenes, Laërce, *Vitae philosophorum* 6; J. Zwicker, *Fontes Historiae Religionis Celticae* (Berlin, 1934), vol 1, pp. 96–97.

[17]Le Roux and Guyonvarc'h, *Les Druides*, p. 58, n. 26.

[18]See Édouard Bachellery, *L'Oeuvre poétique de Gutun Owein, barde gallois de la deuxième moitié du XVe siècle* (Paris, 1950).

if Christianity made the text commonplace, it did not empty it of all its substance.

The Irish learned and mastered Latin and Greek and even Hebrew, and that helped them, during the Merovingian and Carolingian periods, to save the classic culture and at the same time to reevangelize Western and Central Europe. They read and wrote glosses to the Latin and Greek grammarians *ad infinitum;* they translated and wrote commentaries on Virgil and Homer; they wrote glosses to the Epistles of Paul; but, as already stated, they were less successful at classical philosophy, and, where the defense of Christian orthodoxy was concerned, Irish theology produced Scotus Erigena.[19]

The Irish were by no means incapable of abstraction or reflection on a very high level; however, at one moment or another, the criteria of reflection or intelligence are not, or are no longer, the same. One day, a *file* enters a monastery and recites to his fellow monks the old narratives of the Gaelic myths that are the weft of the "history" of Ireland. Because nothing that is Irish can be bad, and all that is truly Irish is oral, spoken, sung, recited, but not written, the oral never loses its rights on Celtic land.

It is precisely from this fundamental notion of the oral that most of the Irish narratives or texts, indefatigably recopied from age to age after the time of Saint Patrick, arise. And it is this orality that is the deeper cause of the narratives being transmitted to us often in versions or renditions that were sometimes very different, if not very divergent or littered with gaps, with incomprehensible

---

[19]See, for example, the introduction to the edition of the *Periphyseon* by I. P. Sheldon-Williams in the series of the *Scriptores Latinin Hiberniae* (Dublin: Dublin Institute for Advanced Studies, 1968), vol. 7/1, pp. 1–34.

words or sentences, and even with interpolations or glosses having nothing to do with the initial subject. At the end of the Scandinavian invasions, that is, after a good century and a half of interruption, the monks took up the scribal tradition again, but the language had evolved, and they often had the choice between either recopying without understanding very well, or adapting the language to that of their times by modifying the text. At times, they did not quite know which method to choose.

Teachers and Students

The Colloquy of Two Sages partakes of all these tribulations, qualities, and flaws. In it, one can see especially, on the surface, a formal Christianization that can be annoying, and a simplicity of expression that contrasts with the constant enigmas and the incessant metaphors that pepper the text. Yet one realizes very quickly that nothing is left to chance in this *Colloquy* and that the verbal joust owes nothing to individual whim. A particular question calls for a particular response, and, if by accident the response did not fit the question, a whole process of rebalancing of the dialogue would be necessary. Nevertheless, such an accident does not happen, or if it ever happened, it was not noted in the transcription that we have. Everything here is and still remains the expression of an organized priestly class, aware of its knowledge and authority, of its importance and its prerogatives. This is so much the case that myth as such is scarcely evoked in the text; rather, it exists only by and for the *filid*, and their archaic and primordial concept of the priest as creator of the cult. This is of little importance, seeing as the gods of Ireland were not, as it were, here first.

One of the most expressive and most significant passages

of the *Colloquy* is the one in which the young Nede defines himself as a descendent of the goddess Dana, with the inevitable symbolic play on words between *dán*, "art," and *Dana*, the name of the mother of the gods of Ireland, the three gods of Dana. The druids and the *filid* are the first *aes dána*, or "people of art," it being well understood that whoever is part of the *aes dána* is a holder of intellectual or technical knowledge or know-how. This art is complementary to "understanding" *(eolas)* and to science *(fis)*. Artisans, blacksmiths, carpenters are also part of the *aes dána* who are Ireland's elite.[20]

The term is laudatory and descriptive; apparently specific to "artisans," it can also serve to indicate, owing to its specializations, the whole priestly class. It is because he is part of the *aes dána* that Lugh is admitted to Tara at the beginning of the narrative of the *Cath Maighe Tuireadh*, or "Second Battle of Magh Tuireadh."[21] It is as *aes dána* that the three druids, or royal *filid* of Conchobar, take part in the great military parade of the Ulates in the narrative of the *Cattle Raid of Cooley*."[22] The existence of the *aes dána* is wholly recognized by the laws of Ireland.[23] All of this, and the teaching that flows from it, obviously owes nothing to Christianity.

---

[20] See p. 103, note 138.

[21] See the *Textes mythologiques irlandais*, vol. 1, pp. 50–52; the Welsh equivalent is in the tale of Culhwch and Olwen when Culhwch presents himself at Arthur's court and is told that only a king's son or an artist bringing his art can be received. *Les Mabinogion*, Joseph Loth, ed. (Paris, 1913), vol. 1, pp. 251–60; in another passage (vol. 1, p. 319), it is Cei who is granted entry into a castle because he is a sword sharpener.

[22] See my introduction, *Cattle Raid of Cooley*, pp. 240 and 243–45; and one of the most important poets of the court of Ulster, Amairgen, is the son of a blacksmith!

[23] *Ancient Laws of Ireland* (Dublin, 1865–1901), vol. 2, p. 118; vol. 3, p. 48; vol. 4, p. 94 §2.

By way of comparison—which will easily speak for itself—here is the extraordinary and archaic passage from the *Cormac's Glossary* (from the beginning of the tenth century!) in which, in discussing a flounder and a kneading trough, a *file* of high rank somewhat cruelly ridicules the student of a colleague. The text is of even more interest given that the *file* in question is named Cruitine, which is precisely the name of the brother of Nede, the too-young candidate to the throne of doctor of Ireland.

Leithech means two things: First, it is the name of a species of fish, so called because of its width and its thinness, as this fish becomes very wide in the ocean; second, *Leithech* is also the name of a kneading trough where dough is spread, as Cruitine said once while going to the home of another poet with his servant, a student who had the pride of a master. Cruitine himself remained outside and let his servant go request hospitality in the poet's house. A pork stomach had been given to him in a cauldron: the poet began to converse with the student, all the while preparing the meal. He noticed the immense pride of the student and the smallness of his intelligence. When the stomach was cooked, he said in the student's presence, *tofotha tarr téin*, that is, "It is time to take it off the fire," to see what kind of response the student would give him because he had heard Cruitine praising the marvelous perfections of the other, as if he were talking about himself. He did not believe him, and this is why he said *tofotha tarr téin*. Three times he said *tofotha tarr téin* and the student answered not a word. Then the student left, went to find Cruitine and he told him the news, that is, the question that the poet had asked, *tofotha tarr téin*. "Very well," said Cruitine, "when he says that to you again, answer him *toe lethaig foen friss ocus fris adaind indlis,* that is, 'put a kneading trough underneath it and light a candle [to see if the stomach is cooked].'" When the student was again seated in the house, the poet said the same thing and the student answered "*toe lethaig,* etc." "Very well," said the poet, "it is not the mouth of a student that returns such an answer. He who returned it is very close by. Cruitine is near. Call him in from outside." So Cruitine was called in, he was welcomed, and other food was put in the cauldron. The pride of the student was small because the poet ridiculed him in conversing with Cruitine.[24]

This whole passage turns on the necessity of identifying the speaker by verifying the pertinence of his answers. The words of an unknown person are by definition worthless until he is identified, and his silences are even more severely judged. But, once the speaker is identified, recognized, and provided with his titles, even if it is through the answers of his simple, not overly gifted student who is of limited intelligence and who is ridiculed by others, he is received with all the respect due his rank. The verification here is the work of a true teacher demonstrating the depth and subtlety of his erudition. Too bad for us if, like the student, we do not grasp all the nuances.

Thus we have an example that is still relatively comprehensible of what Ireland called *berla filid,* the "language of the poets," which was accessible only to the initiated and incomprehensible to everyone else, not so much the rest of humanity but the rest of the Gaelic race, kings and warriors included, who had to be content with the few meager

---

[24]Whitley Stokes, *Three Irish Glossaries* (London, 1862), p. 27.

crumbs that the "initiated" were willing to explain to them. Here, we will no longer have to be content with crumbs. But, in order to have passed through this elementary stage, a little patience was required, as well as some lexicographical or lexical research, the details of which need not concern the reader.

But what was the grade of the *file* Cruitine's student? The "other" poet, whom the archaic text neglected to name, as well as Cruitine himself, are without doubt people at the top of the hierarchy: *ollam*, or "doctors." The student, however, to be treated thus, must have been at the apprentice level. The brief text of *Cormac's Glossary* cannot be understood otherwise, and *The Colloquy of Two Sages* can only be understood as an illustration of the druidic hierarchy, not administrative but traditional, based on the degree and extent of one's learning. It is noteworthy that the first justificatory text of this hierarchy would be legal in essence, and it will be cited fully here, leaving it to the reader to appreciate the subtlety of the nuances. Ireland was very concerned with respect for titles and distance as well as respect for fees and for the consideration owed to all dignitaries. At the same time we very nearly learn the essence of what we need to know about the *filid* and, through a few analogical etymologies that we are not obliged to accept, about the manner in which they understood themselves. Here, we also encounter, fairly often, explanations for certain expressions or metaphors used in the *Colloquy*:

> The seven established degrees of wisdom are: a great sage and a sage, the brilliant wave and the wave of the rock, the illuminator, the interrogator, and the student.
>
> The great sage, as for him, has three names: great sage, doctor, and sage of letters. The doctor is also in the

house in the middle because it is he who is in the house next to the king. A great sage never lacks the answer to a question on the four parts of wisdom [. . .]. His suite is composed of twenty-four people. A seventh of the price of his death is owed to him for refusing him food [that is, a seventh of the price of compensation to be paid to the family in the case of murder].

The teacher of letters. There are three things that raise him to the rank of the compensation due to a provincial king: to be in sync with and in the middle of his students receiving his teaching. He is the man to whom his compensation fee is not paid if he says or teaches nonsense because he is well versed in penance and in the law.

The brilliant wave *(anruth)* now. He is thus named for four reasons: due to the brilliance of his teaching, due to his numerous intellectual qualities, due to the eloquence of his language, due to the extent of his science; because he composes in each area of science—poetry, literature, and its synchronism [what the *Book of Conquests* calls synchronism is the concordance of biblical history with the mythical events of Ireland's "history"]; but he has not yet reached the height of science. His suite is composed of twelve people.

The sage is a man who teaches the fourth part of science, whatever it is, as per Cennfaeladh: "an excellent sage in canon law, due to his fine and good nobility." The number of his people is eight individuals; the price of his compensation is seven *cumal* ["woman slaves"].

The wave of the rock *(sruth do aill)*. The method of this wave is to drown everything that is small, slight, and weak. It carries away blocks of rock that take on the appearance of sand in the heat of the atmosphere. Thus behaves the man who is compared to it: he drowns bad students whom he confounds by the blocks of his testimony and intelligence. He is capable of adapting his teaching to the information in consideration of those people of only slight instruction who recoil in the presence of a noble wave.

The illuminator is the man who responds to his guardian with the intelligence of a doctor. His compensation fee is three demi-*cumal*. He explains the meanings of all the difficulties due to the excellence of his judgment and the brilliance of his intelligence.

The interrogator is one who interrogates his guardian with the intelligence of a doctor. His fee is one demi-*cumal*.

In this way, the degrees of science and church are similar, corresponding to the grades of the poets and the scholars. But for them science is the mother of all the arts and it is from her hand that they all drink.

The seven grades of the *file: éces, anruth, clí, cana, dos, mac fuirmidh, fochloc*.

File ("seer"): that is, *fialshai* (noble wisdom), that is, that wisdom comes from him, for what is noble in him, is understanding, or the teaching in the common language. It is from him that come the pupil, the philosopher, the poet and poetry, or *fili*, that is, *fi* and *li*, *fi* ("come") from his satires and *li* ("brilliant") from his art.

The doctor: he protects many. He is the one who teaches the four areas of poetry and his number of people is the greatest and his protection is greater than all the other grades. Or, doctor *(ollam)*: great is the company *(oll a dam)*: twenty-four people. For there exist three doctors: the doctor of wisdom, the sage of all understanding, and this is why he is appealed to: what he is asked, he refuses not. Neither does there come from him any unresolved difficulties in the judgments of fathers and grandfathers. Or, doctor *(ollam)*: greater *(uille)* is the number of those who are under his protection than under the protection of the other grades. Or, great doctor, the one who binds and is not bound. How is this? Response: as per the king of Connaught, thus is it said: he is not a great doctor *(ni ollam nard)* of the province of Ailill, son of Mata Mor. Or, doctor who protects many *(oll do eim)* whoever is without nobility in the understanding of the grades. The doctor of poetry teaches the four parts of poetry without being unaware of any of them.

Noble wave *(anruth)*, that is, he binds and is not bound like the king who took over Ireland.

The noble wave, this is the beautiful wave of praise which comes from him and the wave of wealth that goes toward him.

Clí: that is, that the nature of pillars is to be strong and straight. The *clí* raises and is raised; it protects and is protected; it is powerful from the very threshold of the house. Thus is this grade in the house of poetry: his art is strong and his judgment is straight in the circuit of his profession. He raises his dignity above those who are inferior to him because his art protects all that exists, from the brilliant wave *(anruth)* to the apprentice *(fochloc)*.

Dos: it is because of his resemblance to a tree that he is named, that is, through the name of a tree they learn their art. It is in the same way through the name of a tree and due to his resemblance that he is called *dos*. For the one-year-old tree is a *dos* that has four leaves. The suite of the *dos* is thus four people.

Mac fuirmid ("son of apprenticeship"): he is a boy who is trained in the art from his childhood; or, it is his art that is his son. It is not good that he has a grade, but he is a good son of [. . . ?].

Fochloc ("apprentice)": he is named for his resemblance to a sprig of cress having two leaves. He thus has for his suite two people; or, *fochloc* is a hardened shoot, without growth of art, or his art is slight due to his youth.[25]

We have in this passage, among other things, the only insular texts in which it is stated that the druid binds and is not bound. This explains in particular the workings of the interdictions to which the king is subject.[26]

Here now is the hierarchical list of the legal treatise of the *Senchus Mor,* or "Great Antiquity," concerning the restrictions, effected by Saint Patrick in the fifth century, on the activities of the *filid.* It is at the same time an explanation of the principles of the Christianization of Ireland:

But Patrick abolished these three things among the poets when they believed, as they were profane rites, for the Teinm Laegha nor the Imus Forosna could not be performed by them without offering to the idol gods. He did not leave them after this any rite in which offering should be made to the devil, for their profession was pure. And he left them after this extemporaneous recital, because it was acquired through great knowledge and application, and also the registering of the genealogies

---

[25]*Ancient Laws of Ireland,* vol. 4, pp. 354–60.

[26]See my *Magie, médecine et divination chez les Celtes,* chapter 3 on "La parole du druide," pp. 89–177.

of the men of Erin, and the artistic rules of poetry, and the Duili Sloinnte and the Duili Fedha, and story-telling with lays, viz., the Ollamh, with his seven times fifty stories, the Anruth with his thrice fifty and half fifty, the Clí with his eighty, the Cana with his sixty, the Dos with his fifty, the Mac Fuirmid with his forty, the Fochluc with his thirty, the Drisac with his twenty, the Taman with his ten stories, and the Oblaire with his seven stories. These were the chief stories and the minor stories. The chief stories that they repeated, treated of demolitions, cattle spoils, courtships, battles, killings, combats, elopements, feasts, encampments, adventures, tragedies, and plunderings.[27]

There are two kinds of *scéla*, or "narratives," the *primscéla*, or "primary narratives," and the *foscéla*, or "secondary narratives." But both were told at night to the kings and the great lords of the main courts of Ireland.

As for the fees paid to the *filid* of Ireland, they are proportional to the circumstances and to the hierarchy of knowledge. Here are those of the *ollam*, or "doctor":

The poet-doctor: the price for his honor is seven woman-slaves. The name of his poetic composition is *anamain cain chaithiriach*, with the four perfections that it unites within itself, that is, *nath*, *laid*, and *camain*. Ten cows and a heifer are paid for the body of the *anamain* poem, five cows for a *nath*, two cows and a heifer for an *anair*, two cows for an *emain*, one cow for a *laid*, and that

---

[27] *Ancient Laws of Ireland*, vol. 1, pp. 45–47; cf. Le Roux and Guyonvarc'h, *Les Druides*, pp. 50–53. On the divinatory incantations, see again Guyonvarc'h, *Magie, médicine et divination chez les Celtes*, chapter 7 on "Divination," pp. 271–322.

makes a total of twenty-one cows. His total escort is twenty-four people for a night of entertainment and for a visit to the sick; ten for common necessities; ten for a night of feasting; eight in a circuit made to claim debts and contracts. His complete protection is of one month for food and service. He has seven times fifty stories, two-sevenths of them being secondary stories and five-sevenths primary stories.[28]

I insist as well on clarifying more precisely the notion of specialization because it is scarcely discernable in the reading of the *Colloquy*, yet it is indispensable to an exact understanding of the notion of the priestly class among the Celts. The word *druid* is in fact a general designation to which any member of the priestly class is entitled. The *file*, or Irish "poet," is already a specialization of the druid; the *vate*, or "seer" (Gallic *vatis*, Irish *fáith*), is another. But inside these two categories other specializations appear: teacher, lawyer, storyteller, historian, satirist, harpist, wine waiter, doorman or porter, doctor, architect, and so on, which have been studied in detail.[29] It is important to add here, to ensure proper comprehension of the *Colloquy*, that a druid, or a *file*, can possibly have at his disposal several specializations. It is rare that a druid be not at the same time a satirist, storyteller, and historian, and even a lawyer as well, and sometimes a seer. Only medicine and music seem to call for special gifts or skills. Let's not forget that the druid, or the *file*, assists the king in the exercising of his

---

[28]*Ancient Laws of Ireland*, vol. 1, p. 58; cf. Le Roux and Guyonvarc'h, *Les Druides*, p. 53.

[29]*Les Druides*, p. 44 ff.

power and that he is frequently called upon to play the role of seer, lawyer, and teacher. All this certainly goes back to Indo-European origins.[30]

Form and Content of
The Colloquy of Two Sages

In another unusual occurrence in a Gaelic text, the form of the *Colloquy* is part of the visible intentions of the writer or the transcriber. A preamble of ten short paragraphs explains how Nede, a disciple living with a master in Scotland, learns of the death of his father, Adna, while listening to the moaning of an ocean wave, and returns to Emain Macha in Ulster in the company of his three brothers. As part of the archaic Irish narrative tradition, we are told about three minor interrogatory episodes concerning the names of the foxglove (digitalis), reed, and sanicle, which cause temporary returns to the master's home. But these three minor episodes are proof that for a *file,* whatever his rank, there should not be any questions that his ignorance might keep him from answering. He should know everything; if he doesn't, he cannot be initiated. Another purely Irish and Celtic detail is in the enumeration of the places that punctuate the route of the voyage from Scotland back to Ulster. This kind of information, which at times reaches tedious lengths, is in this case the consequence of customary practice and not a necessity inherent to the text. There are no recitations, narratives, or annals that avoid this device. In any case, a catalog such as this one is sometimes useful; what we learn from the first paragraph is that the identity of the northern locale

---

[30]See, among others, Enrico Campanile, Chatia Orlandi, and Saverio Sani, "Fuzione e figura del poeta nella cultura celtica e indiana," *Studi e saggi linguistici*" 14 (Pisa, 1974), pp. 228–51; Enrico Campanile, *Ricerche di cultura poetica indoeuropea* (Pisa, 1977).

that is the place of teaching and initiation is Scotland, whose Gaelic name, Alba, means "white."[31]

There follows information on the grade that Nede has already reached, which is identifiable thanks to the silver rod. Then comes the encounter with Bricriu and his lie, which misleads Nede regarding the vacancy of the seat of the foremost doctor of Ireland. It is interesting to note that Nede's error is quickly corrected by Ferchertne. There is, at the beginning, a literal usurpation by Nede of the seat left vacant by his father's death, for the title is earned at the minimum by a test or a kind of contest—it is not inherited. And so Nede does not persist and immediately agrees to undergo the examination.

Thus the *Colloquy* opens with questions that are equally interrogations. It will be noticed that each time Ferchertne asks a more difficult question than the one preceding, and that, in answering the question, each time Nede's responses are more difficult to understand. It is thus also a true test of Nede's capacity to agree, to recognize, with sufficient good graces, the superiority of the master. In other words, the Irish professorial code of conduct is perfectly safe and professionally justified.

Ferchertne has never heard of Nede as a doctor of Ireland (lines 1–9). The first argument is fairly meager: Nede would be an apprentice (which he is not, in fact; the grade of *anruth* being pretty high as it is!), and he has grass for a beard (proof of his youth, which is not a valid judgment on his potential intelligence). Further, Ferchertne has never heard of Nede (obviously there had not been enough time for Nede to have made a name for himself on account of his age, which, furthermore, is not specified!). The latter

---

[31]See pp. 74–75, nn. 8 and 9.

answers that it is the sage's responsibility to instruct the ignorant, which he does not do for the moment (ll.10–21).

Next comes the question, "Where did you come from?" Nede answers with several metaphors explaining that the sage's teaching defends truth, fights against falsehood, and renews poetry (ll.24–36). Ferchertne responds in turn with geographical metaphors that only someone very familiar with Irish mythology would be able to understand (ll.37–43).

Then comes the personal question, "What is your name?" Nede answers with a series of definitions full of imagery that, in effect, can be applied to the personality of a poet (ll.46–56). Ferchertne uses less imagery and more complex definitions (ll.59–66).

Then comes the technical question, "What art do you practice?" That is, of what are you capable? Nede's answers are allusions to the power of poetry and its diverse qualities (ll.69–81); Ferchertne's answers to Nede on the same question are more refined, but are the same kind of metaphors, defining the science of a poet (ll.83–102).

The interrogation then flows as one might expect; Ferchertne asks, "What have you undertaken?" All of Nede's responses are metaphors that could be applied to poetic activity (ll.105–15); Ferchertne's answers apply to the same theme, but are a little more difficult (ll.116–24).

Then follows the question, "What route did you take?" Nede's answers can no longer be immediately understood (ll.126–35); Ferchertne's are comprised of mythological allusions, each of which calls for explanation or commentary (ll.138–45).

The next-to-last question is, "Whose son are you?" Nede manages the situation magnificently by using a sort of intellectual genealogy in the royal Irish style, which ties him, outside of all Christian orthodoxy, to the three gods of Dana (ll.148–58). Ferchertne's responses are much more abstract and enigmatic, falling well within the Celtic propensity for the mysterious and the contradictory (ll.160–68). These answers emphasize the intemporality of the druid whose knowledge is beyond life and death and, in a way, inherent in all endings and all beginnings; the man who has been and who was not born simultaneously transcends both being and nonbeing (which has nothing to do with nothingness!).

All that remains now is the final question to be asked, the question that, in the courts of Ireland, is commonly asked of the *file* who is requested to say what he knows or what he has learned, and especially to recount something that will interest everyone—"Do you have any news?" The "news" in question here is rendered by a very particular Irish word, *scéla* (Modern Irish *scéala*), which means "tale," or "narrative," as well as "news" in the sense of an event that happened far away or that has just happened. It is, further, "information," as well as the relation between a whole chain of events. In reality, the *scéla*, whose linguistic roots are tied to the general meaning of "say," refer to all that a *file* is capable of holding in his memory and of saying, without great distinction between the nature or the type.

And the two *filid*, each according to his own concerns, will answer the question contradictorily. The younger one, who here plays the role of disciple, will enumerate the "good" news (ll.170–93), and the older one, the master, will save for himself the "bad" news. And this will be the longest part of the text (ll.195–310).

The *Colloquy* now comes to an end and the conclusion arrives, necessary, inevitable, and relatively brief: the young *file* recognizes the superiority—both hierarchical (or spiritual) and intellectual—of his elder, on behalf of whom he removes his father's robe (ll.312–17).

Finally, as a postscript to Nede's adventures, or to his *curriculum vitae*, let us refer, though it is not directly related to the *Colloquy*, to the final episode of his life as told in *Cormac's Glossary*. After his father's death, Nede was adopted by his uncle, Caier, the king of Connaught. Nede transgresses the rules of his *file*-hood and commits adultery with the queen. Then, at the queen's instigation, he unjustly satirizes his uncle in order to occupy the throne in his place. Caier dies of shame, but a rock explodes and a fragment penetrates Nede's eye, which is standard punishment for a druid who is unjust and who has seriously erred, against both priesthood and royalty.[32]

The Prophecies of the *File*

The good news related by Nede is unmistakably less significant in terms of both length and consequences. Its scope is *grosso modo* limited to announcing peace and material abundance. This brings to mind the description of Ireland's prosperity under the reign of King Conn:

> Conn had been at this time thirty-five years as Ireland's king, for his sovereignty over Ireland lasted fifty-three years in its entirety. He was the best king of Ireland before faith, for Ireland was never in such improved circumstances but with him, except under the reign of the one

---

[32]See on this last point the complete translation of the text and our analysis in *La Société celtique dans l'idéologie trifonctionnelle et la tradition réligieuse indo-européenne* (Rennes: Ouest-France, 1992), pp. 144–48, and again the reworking of this text from the point of view of incantatory magic, this time in *Magie, médecine et divination chez les Celtes*, pp. 155–59.

and only Cormac, grandson of Conn. It is not known
which of the two reigns was the best, as the poet Senfuath
says in his eulogy of the two kings. Thus was the sovereignty of Conn: without pillage, without stealing, without
need, without sickness, without fleas, without flies, without mosquitoes, without dampness, without great winds,
without snow, excepting three things, dew, rain, and fog;
without wasps, without hornets, excepting the bees of
Tara's foliage, without dead trees, without violence to anyone, without victory songs, without sighing, without
extortion, without unemployed men, without watchmen,
without troubles. During all this time Ireland had not one
season without fruits, not one night without dew, not one
night without warmth. Every tree was fresh, every river
was full of fish as soon as the water reached knee height.
There was neither spear nor knife nor sword; the only
weapons were rods and goads. The land was worked only
fifteen days a month in spring and it produced three times
the grain per year. On the horns of cows the cuckoos sang
their song. There were a hundred clusters per branch and
a hundred nuts per cluster, nine furrows per ear of wheat.
The calves were milk cows before their usual time. The
price was an ounce of shining silver for twelve bushels of
wheat and twelve pails of honey. The weight of each
ounce was twenty-four scruples, and this was what one cow
was worth. Ireland was alike to paradise, and she was a land
of promise with flowers full of honey, under the reign of
Conn of the Hundred Battles, so says Eochaid Ecius:

> Conn of the Hundred Battles, his reign
> lasted fifty-three years,
> without devastation, without fires,
> without the murder of living men,

> *without pillage, without stealing, without need to anyone,*
> *without illness cruel or short,*
> *without fleas, without mosquitoes acting together,*
> *without ghastly flies,*
> *without the wetness of downpours, without great winds,*
> *without snow, noble battles,*
> *but only these three things together:*
> *dew, rain, and fog.*[33]

Most noteworthy in this Edenic state is the absence of weapons, the "rod" being the magic instrument of the druids and the "goad" what the charioteer uses to drive the horses of war chariots.

A comparison can be drawn with the brief prophecy contained in the two quatrains in which the *file* Amairgen Glungel ("of the white knee"), disembarking from his ship in Ireland, promises his Gaelic countrymen all the riches of the sea:

> *Sea full of fish,*
> *fertile lands,*
> *abundance of fish,*
> *clouds of birds,*
> *rugged sea . . .*
>
> *white hail*
> *with hundreds of salmon,*
> *great whales,*
> *port songs,*
> *abundance of fish,*
> *Sea full of fish . . .*[34]

---

[33]*Arne Fingen,* "La veillée de Fingen," *Textes mythologiques irlandais,* p. 194, § 15.
[34]*Textes mythologiques irlandais,* vol. 1, p. 15.

What Nede offers us is in the same vein but much less elaborate: material prosperity, abundance of fish and harvests, peace, pleasant weather. But whereas in the text and the short poem of the *Arne Fingen* the abundance of prosperity is negatively rendered as the absence of war and disaster, and as the needlessness of all priestly or military functions—because the need for these latter being no longer felt—Nede's brief (definitely lacunar) list in the *Colloquy* has a positive slant and, without envisioning any era, it enters, on the list of good news—which, by the way, is not false—wisdom, abundance of art, and full military worth. The three classes, priestly, military, and productive, collaborate thus in the social and religious harmony under the direction of the druids. Which opinion is best? It is likely that neither one is superior to the other and that, according to the case at hand, the *file* commentator could pass, or might have passed, from one to the other. Let us not forget that here contradictions never become absolute and irreconcilable opposites. Let us not forget either what has already been discussed, namely that the druids and the *filid* are, technically, *aes dána*, or "people of art," akin to carpenters or blacksmiths. Their religious function certainly classifies them, whereas their scholarly skill qualifies them. In Ireland, whoever is the holder of a particular kind of knowledge or know-how, in other words of an "art" in the medieval sense of the word, is respected and honored. This is why even a blacksmith can hold the title of "doctor."

It is possible, finally, that the narrative of the *Fingen's Vigil* sees Conn Cet Chathach as a mythical king, whereas the transcriber of the *Colloquy*, when he touches upon Nede's misadventures, thinks pseudohistorically in a way, and within a social and religious reality that for him is concrete. This in turn suffices to justify a posteriori the few references to mythological characters unamenable to Christianization, the Túatha dé Dánann in general—the three gods of Dana and divinities such as Lugh, Nuada, the Mac Oc (son of Dagda)—or the Boand in particular, without omitting Bricriu, whose intervention, at the beginning of the narrative of Nede's adventures, further suffices to situate the *Colloquy* definitively as in the category of epic as well as that of myth, as thus at the antipodes of history.

But it is almost certain that all these formulae and names of ancient Irish divinities were part of the supply of traditional knowledge required of the *file* once he had reached a certain grade, and it is also just as certain that the written transmission did not enrich its content—much to the contrary. Let us be happy it did not deprive us of everything.

The debate, or oratorical joust, concerning the good and bad "news" must have been part of the druidic "exercises" (I cannot find another word!) of scholarship and virtuosity, or it must have, as is the impression here, even served as a "test of passage" in order for the *file* to gain access to a higher grade or to have the right to lay claim to a new master, a higher rank.

The most important part of the *Colloquy* is therefore what is in fact a long monologue of sinister predictions coming from Ferchertne's mouth. The tone is simultaneously strongly marked with prophetism (perhaps millenarian, insofar as the Christian influence is real) and with visionary certainty. It cannot help but correspond to druidic notions about the end of the world or, rather, about what India would call the end of a cycle.

What is remarkable in this sequence, and what contrasts sharply with all the remaining questions and responses, is the very general feel of the definitions or aphorisms. No one is designated by name as being guilty of, or responsible for, the worst disasters, and the whole discourse is steeped in generalities, to which Ireland has hardly accustomed us.

Although fairly hard to classify as a whole, the list can be divided into several categories, roughly defined as follows:

1. the cruelty of the human race;
2. bad judgments;
3. bad chiefs and bad kings;
4. an abundance of usurpers;
5. generalized falsehood and ignorance;
6. an absence of all respect and all honor;
7. the arrogance and pride of the common people;
8. an inversion of the meaning of beauty and art;
9. an absence of all decency or propriety;
10. a nonrespect for and inversion of hierarchies;
11. a breakdown of all the social classes through inversion of positions;
12. the sterility of plants and animals;
13. the inversion of the seasons;
14. the occurrence of atmospheric disasters and epidemics.

The comparison is immediate with the last two paragraphs of *The Second Battle of Magh Tuireadh*, which is the primary Irish mythological narrative. The divinity in question here is the Morrigan ("Great Queen"), or goddess of war:

> Then, after the battle had been won and the bodies remaining from the massacre washed, the Morrigan, daughter of Ernmas, began to announce the battle and the great victory that had been won, to the royal hills of Ireland, to the armies of the *sídhe*, to the principal rivers and their sources. This is also why the Bodb describes these lofty feats. "Do you have any news?" they would ask, and she would answer:

> *"Peace up to the sky,*
> *from sky to earth,*
> *earth under sky,*
> *strength to everyone."*

She also prophesied the end of the world, predicting all the evil that would happen, every sickness, and every vengeance, and she sang the song below:

> *"I see a world that will please me not:*
> *summer without flowers,*
> *cows without milk,*
> *women without modesty,*
> *men without courage,*
> *captives without king;*
>
> *trees without fruit,*
> *sea without spawning;*
> *bad opinion of the old people,*
> *bad judgment of the judges,*
> *every man will be a traitor,*
> *every boy a thief;*
> *the son will go into the father's bed,*
> *the father will go into the son's bed:*
> *every man will be the stepfather of his brother.*
>
> *A bad time:*
> *sons will betray their fathers,*
> *daughters will betray their mothers."*[35]

This is not exactly the same text. The expression is much more concise, and it is above all not Christianized.

---

[35]*Textes mythologiques irlandais*, p. 59, §§ 164–65.

Still, the general sense is absolutely identical and is enough to prove the existence of a carefully transmitted and repeated eschatological tradition.

There is no explicit mention in the *Colloquy*, of the final disaster envisioned by the druids according to Strabo (4.4): "One day fire and water alone will rule."[36] The only allusion to a final tidal wave is contained in paragraph 295: "The sea will invade all lands having residences of the Land of Promise." And it must be specified further that the expression used to mean the Otherworld, "the Land of Promise" (Tir Tairngire), is characteristic of the Christianization of the Irish lexicon, being merely the faithful translation of the evangelical Terra Repromissionis. Neither is the Antichrist overlooked, and his name here is quite curious—Ancríst, literally, the "non-Christ." The text insists on another point as well, a point we rarely think of in the evocation of the end of this world, *the negation or loss of the notion of law* through betrayal, falsity, lying, or breach of the "given" word, that is, promises. This is very close to the old formula of the legal treatise of the *Senchus Mor:* "There are three times when a perishing of the world will happen: the period of the death of men, the increased instance of war, the dissolution of verbal contracts."[37]

The natural disasters marking the end of the world and the coming of the Antichrist are not overlooked. And if Christianization is definite and forever, it is at the same time superficial, since all it is used for is to justify, in the name of the purest Christianity, a notion of social and human relationship that owes nothing to Christianity in any form whatsoever and that, indeed, is completely foreign to it, resting as it does upon the observation of the breakdown of human

---

[36]See *Les Druides*, p. 336.

[37]*Ancient Laws of Ireland*, vol. 3, p. 12.

relationships and functions in comparison to the state of affairs at the beginning of the mythological age, which is an entirely traditional manner of viewing the devolution of societies. The modern illusion of the twofold "progress" of technology and intelligence was never used in medieval Ireland. For traditional *filid*, the evolution of humanity is that of a progressive distancing, accelerating with time, from an initial Edenic state in which the perfection of the *síd*, the Irish Otherworld, suffices to make all hierarchies useless and to avoid the use of technologies in the service of evil. But fundamentally—and fortunately—since fire and the wheel, man has invented only improvements to the details.

Even more than negation, it is the inversion of hierarchies that, added to untruth, cruelty, and ignorance, engenders chaos, and, when its time comes, the death of human societies, which are no longer led by capable chiefs or kings but by usurpers, liars, thieves, and worthless people. Technocracy was yet to be invented. This point of view has nothing obviously unusual about it, and it would be easy to find it in all eras—even in ours—in the works of philosophers or thinkers, sociologists of all stripes, and even theologians of all denominations who express an opinion on their contemporaries.

All the inversions or negations of human hierarchies can be found in the transformation of the elements. This transformation is not complete and relentless annihilation; it is a change of one nature into its opposite: mountains will become plains, peat bogs will become fields of flowers, horse dung will become the color of gold, and water will taste like wine (ll.299–305), with, it is implied, a sad tinge of illusion.

In the Celtic notion of the world and time, however, the archaism of the *Colloquy* is obvious by its limitations. The macrocosm is reduced to Ireland, and the time is solely that of apocalyptic disasters that will strike the island in an unspecified future. Undoubtedly, divine "time" is not measurable in terms of human time, but all Christian millenarian prophecies tend to set a date relatively close to the era in which they are expressed. Such is not the case here; the only bit of dating having any precision is the announcement that Ireland will be abandoned seven years before Judgment Day (l.295). It is not said that she will be annihilated or relocated to Scandinavia. Neither is it said that after the end of the cycle there will be a renewing or a sort of remission, more or less lasting, before the final annihilation. It is regrettable above all that, if the divinities of the Túatha dé Dánann, that is, the pre-Christian gods of Ireland, are sometimes named in metaphors, their destiny as divine entities—who are themselves subjected to the process of the breakdown of the world—is not envisioned at any time in the *Colloquy*. This missing piece is certainly owing to the Christianization of the text, and it is irremediable. We have a complete lack, in the Celtic language, of the equivalent—which did exist—of the Germanic Götterdämmerung.

Then, abruptly, as if all that were nothing but a school exercise in the manner of the Greek rhetoricians who were trained to prove a truth one day and its contrary the next, everything is clarified by a final game of question and answer. First, Nede recognizes the existence of a hierarchy. He knows God, then immediately after God, his "hazel tree of poetry," the "great poet and seer," Ferchertne. This second proposition is suspicious. As a sign of humility and submission, he kneels in front of Ferchertne and strips off his father's robe. Of passing note is the expression "great poet and seer" *(rofili faith)*, which specifies the functional specialization of the poet in spite of all the marks of Christianization.

Next, Ferchertne, in his comprehensive and definitive response, in essence promises his disciple, who probably was not asking for this much, what could be called a bright professional future (ll.318–24) according to Celtic norms, in particular that he would be a "vessel for poetry," a "rock for the doctors," and, above all, "the arm of a king," which would only make sense previous to the conversion of Ireland to Christianity. This last goes to prove, if there was any need, the fundamental antiquity of the *Colloquy*.

Finally, the spiritual filiation reclaimed by Nede is genuinely in keeping with the Celtic notion of the transmission of knowledge and understanding.[38]

In closing I would like to mention briefly another text, concerning a different subject, but which is also direct proof of the unflagging intellectual activity of the *filid* of Ireland. It is a treatise on the privileges, rights, and responsibilities of the poets. It is also a collection of anecdotes and adventures, more than it is a legal and theoretical treatise, which is why it is not part of the present study. Besides, there is another, less noble reason why no one, until now, has been interested in it.

The text is contained in manuscript H.2.15B, pp. 135–56, at Trinity College, Dublin. It is attributed to a well-known scribe, Dubhaltach Mac Firbhisigh, and a first copy of it was made, probably toward the middle of the nineteenth century, by Eugene O'Curry, who in his time was a professor at the University of Dublin. But since 1940 the manuscript has been extremely fragile, and as a result the text is badly damaged.

It was published in its entirety by E. J. Gwynn, as "An Old-Irish Tract on the Privileges and Responsibilities of Poets" (*Eriu* 13 [Dublin, 1940], pp. 1–60). The language is clearly identifiable as a fairly curiously transcribed Old Irish, of the seventeenth century, in the pre–Modern Irish style of writing. But the difficulty is such that the editor

---

[38]See below, pp. 75–76, n. 14.

himself balked in the face of the painstaking scholarly work that such a translation represented. He wrote: "I must freely confess that a great part of the text is to me quite unintelligible, and that there is much more of which I can only dimly discern the meaning; while the want of apparent connexion between consecutive paragraphs does not tend to make the general drift easier to follow."[39]

The important thing in this case, however, is that we be aware of a text that is, with and in spite of its obscurities, another aspect of the activity and the reflection of the druids of Ireland. Nevertheless, this text does not at all concern a dialogue between a master and a student.

At the beginning of this introduction I noted that there was no other text comparable to *The Colloquy of Two Sages*, though I did mention the *Colloquy of the Elders*, which is very different. After an in-depth examination of the content of the text and the pertinent glosses, this observance can only be repeated. After the treatise of privileges just mentioned, I know of no other text, whether the various interviews with the druid Mog Ruith in the narrative of the *Siege of Druim Damhghaire*, or of the two swineherd druids in the narrative of the *Conception of the Two Swineherds*. None of these texts clearly relates to the teaching, the knowledge, and the hierarchies of the priestly class. Once more, and in conclusion, I maintain that *The Colloquy of Two Sages* is a unique text. And because of this it is all the more precious.[40]

In the appendix is found a pedagogical text, the counsel lavished upon a king by the great hero of Ulster, Cúchulainn.

---

[39]*Eriu* 13 (1940), p. 1.

[40]Fragments of my translation of the text of the *Colloguy* have been published, under my name, by Mr. Jean-Phillipe de Tonnac, *L'Occident en quête des sens* (Paris: Maisonneuve-Laroze, 1996), pp. 255–58, under the title "Ce n'est pas difficile." But these excerpts include no notes.

The list is included in the narrative of the *Serglige Concu-laind*, or "Sickness of Cúchulainn." But these precepts are more recommendations than restrictive teachings. The reader will thus see more clearly the difference between a priestly-type teaching—done entirely by suggestion, metaphor, comparison, and innuendo—and the direct and obligatory teaching of precepts and of rules of political codes of conduct intended for a future king. The reader will also see that Celtic scholars were far from being without lessons of wisdom whether given or received, and neither did they lag behind any of the peoples of the ancient world in terms of the care they brought to the spiritual, intellectual, and moral education of their youth in general and of their students in particular. Their pedagogy is at times likely to surprise or amaze us. We must not forget that since antiquity, and even more so since the Renaissance—not to mention even our own era—practical pedagogy of all kinds and degrees has changed multiple times in terms of form, principles, and appearances, if not in means and, at times, aims.

What can be drawn from this, finally, is a certainty, some eternal evidence in the eyes of those who have practiced, at whatever level, the difficult job of teaching, and that is that the best of the pedagogies, even the Socratic method, is ineffective against foolishness and that the most rigid or the most execrable pedagogy has never hindered an intelligent student from learning, especially where a future initiate is concerned. This is what was known, well before us, by all the druids of Gaul, Brittany, and Ireland.

Immacallam
in dá Thúarad

The Colloquy of Two Sages

Immacallam in dá Thúarad

THE COLLOQUY OF TWO SAGES[1]

§ 1. Adne,[2] son of Uthider, of the people[3] of Connaught,[4] [was] a doctor[5] of Ireland in science and poetry.[6] He had a son, namely Nede.[7] This son went, then, to learn science in Scotland,[8] at the home of Eochu Echbel,[9] and he stayed with Eochu until he became accomplished in science.

§ 2. One day, the boy went down to the seaside, for the poets deemed the seaside to be always a place of revelation of science. The boy heard a noise in the waves, that is, a plaintive and sad song,[10] and this seemed strange to him. So the boy put a spell[11] on the waves until they showed him what it was about. After that, it was explained to him that the waves were mourning his father after his death, [12] that his robe had been given to the *file* Ferchertne, and that he, Ferchertne, had taken[13] the position of doctor in place of Nede's own father, Adne.

§ 3. The boy went to his house and told [this] to his guardian,[14] namely Eochaid. And he [Eochaid] said to him: "Go now to your country. Our two sciences cannot be kept in a single place,[15] for your science clearly showed you that you are a doctor in knowledge."[16]

§ 4. So Nede left, and with him his three brothers, namely Lugaid, Cairbre, Cruttine.[17] They came across a stalk of foxglove on their path. One of them said: Why is this called foxglove [digitalis]? As they did not know, they returned to Eochaid's house and were with him for one month. They started out again. They came across a reed. One of them said: Why is this called a reed? As they did not know, they returned to their guardian's house. They left his home at the end of another month. They came across a stalk of sanicle. As they didn't know why this was called a sanicle stalk, they returned to Eochaid's and they were with him for another month.[18]

§ 5. When these questions had been resolved for them, they left for Cantire and he went after that to Rind Snoc. From Port Rig, they next passed over the sea and reached Rind Roisc. Next [they passed] through Semne, Latharna, Mag Line, Ollarba, Tulach Roisc, Ard Slebe, Craeb Selcha, Mag Ercaite, on the Bann, along the Uachtar, through Glenn Rige, through the districts of Huy Bresail, through Ard Sailech, which today is called Armagh, through the Sidbruig of Emain.[19]

§ 6. So this is how the boy went, [with] a silver branch above him, for this is what was above the *anruth*. [There was], however, a gold branch above the doctors. [There was, however,] a bronze branch above the other poets.[20]

§ 7. They then set out for Emain Macha.[21] Then they met Bricriu[22] in the meadow.[23] He told them that, if they gave him his fee, Nede would be a doctor of Ireland through his counsel and intercession. Nede gave him a purple tunic with gold and silver ornament. Bricriu told him then to go sit in the doctor's place, and he told him that Ferchertne[24] was dead, whereas he was north of Emain, guiding the wisdom of his students.[25]

§ 8. And Bricriu said then that a beardless man could not secure the position of doctor in Emain Macha for he [Nede] was childish as far as age was concerned. Nede took a good handful of grass and put a spell on it such that everyone thought he had a beard.[26] He went and sat on the doctor's seat and wrapped his robe around him. The robe was of three colors, that is, the color of brilliant birds in the middle, a shower of white bronze on the lower part, and the brilliance of gold on the upper part.[27]

§ 9. After this, Bricriu went to Ferchertne and he said to him: "It would be a shame for you if you are ousted from the position of doctor today. An honorable young man has taken the doctor's place in Emain." Ferchertne was angry and he entered the royal house such that he was on the threshold, his hand on the [door] jamb. He then said: "Who is this poet, the poet . . . ?"[28]

§ 10. The site of this dialogue is meanwhile Emain Macha. The time of the dialogue is the time of Conchobar, son of Nessa. The author of it is Nede, son of Adne of Connaught, or he is of the people of the goddess Dana, as he says himself in the dialogue: "I am the son of Dan ['poetry'], Dan the son of Osmenad ['attention,' 'care']"[29]—and Ferchertne, poet of the Ulates. The cause of its composition is that the robe of Adne had been given to Ferchertne by Medb and Ailill after the death of Adne. So Nede, son of Adne, came from Scotland as described to Emain and sat in the doctor's throne. Ferchertne entered the house and he said, upon seeing Nede:[30]

1   Who is this poet, this poet around whom is the robe with its splendor?

2   He would reveal himself after having sung some poetry.[31]

3 From what I can see, he is an apprentice.[32]

4 Grass is how he has come by his great beard.[33]

5 At the site of sung music.[34]

6 Who is this poet, poet of dispute?[35]

7 I have not heard anything about the intelligence of the son of Adne.[36]

8 I have not heard [about him] with unfailing knowledge.[37]

9 An error, by [my] letters, is Nede's seat.[38]

9a Here is the honorable response that Nede gave to Ferchertne:[39]

[NEDE SAID]

10 An ancient one, O my elder,[40]

11 each sage is a sage of teaching.[41]

12 A sage is the reproach of all ignorant people.[42]

13 You would see that he knows in advance[43]

14 which reproach, which nature [is within us].[44]

15 Welcome is even the piercing intelligence of wisdom.[45]

16 A young man's failings are slight if his art has not been well interrogated.[46]

17 Follow, master [a more regular approach].[47]

18 You show badly,[48]

19 You have shown badly.[49]

20 You dispense very meagerly the food of science to me.[50]

21 I have sucked the essential juices of a good man, rich in treasures.[51]

[FERCHERTNE SAID]

22 A question, O young man of instruction, where did you come from?[52]

[NEDE SAID]

23 This is not difficult:

24 from the heel of a sage, that is, from the proximity of
    a sage,[53]

25 from a confluence of wisdom,[54]

26 from perfections of goodness,[55]

27 from the brilliance of the rising sun,[56]

28 from hazel trees,[57]

29 from the poetic art,[58]

30 from circuits of splendor,[59]

31 through which the true is measured according to
    excellence,[60]

32 through which the truth is learned,[61]

33 in which the untruth is placed,[62]

34 through which the colors are seen,[63]

35 through which the poems are renewed.[64]

36 And you, O my elder, where did you come from?[65]

[FERCHERTNE ANSWERED]

37 This is not difficult: along the columns of age,[66]

38 along the rivers of Leinster,[67]

39 along the magic hill of the wife of Nechtan,[68]

40 along the forearm of the wife of Nuada,[69]

41 along the land of the sun,[70]

42 along the dwelling place of the moon,[71]

43 along the umbilical cord of the young man.[72]

44 A question, O boy of teaching, what is your name?[73]

[NEDE ANSWERED]

45 This is not difficult:

46 very small,[74]

47 very big,[75]

48 very firm,[76]

49   very brilliant.[77]

50   Ardor of fire.[78]

51   Fire of words.[79]

52   Sound of knowledge.[80]

53   Source of wealth.[81]

54   Sword of singing.[82]

55   Direct art,[83]

56   with the bitterness of fire.[84]

57   And you, O my elder, what is your name?

[FERCHERTNE ANSWERED]

58   This is not difficult:

59   the one closest to the omens,

60   the hero who explains,[85]

61   who tells,

62   who interrogates.

63   Search for science.

64   Weft of art.[86]

65   Vessel for poetry.[87]

66   Abundance coming from the sea.[88]

67   A question, O boy of teaching, what art do you
     practice?

[NEDE ANSWERED]

68   This is not difficult:

69   making faces blush,[89]

70   piercing the flesh,[90]

71   coloring decency,[91]

72   striking impudence,

73   nourishing poetry,[92]

74   seeking renown,

75   courting science,[93]

76   having an art for each mouth,[94]

77 diffusing knowledge,[95]
78 stripping words,[96]
79 in a little room,[97]
80 the cattle of a sage,[98]
81 a river of science,[99]
81a abundance of teaching,[100]
82 delights of kings, lucid narratives.[101]
82a And you, O my elder, what art do you practice?

[FERCHERTNE ANSWERED]

82b This is not difficult:
83 the hunt for aid,[102]
84 to establish peace,[103]
85 to keep order in a troop,[104]
86 tribulation of young men,[105]
87 celebration of the art,
88 a cover with a king.[106]
89 [. . . ? . . .] the Boyne,[107]
90 *briamon smethrach*,[108]
91 Athirne's shield,[109]
92 a share of new wisdom coming from the river of science,[110]
93 color of inspiration,[111]
94 structure of intelligence,[112]
95 art of little poems
96 clear arrangement
97 red narratives,[113]
98 a glorified path,[114]
99 a pearl in the seat[?],[115]
100 rescuing science
101 after a poem,[116]
102 after a poetic composition.[117]

[FERCHERTNE SAID]

103   A question, O boy of teaching, what have you under-
      taken?

[NEDE ANSWERED]

104   This is not difficult:
105   [to go] into the plain of age,
106   into the mountain of youth
107   in pursuit of age,[118]
108   following behind a king,[119]
109   in a dwelling made of clay,[120]
110   between the candle and its head,[121]
111   between the battle and its horror,[122]
112   among the strong men of Tethra,[123]
113   among the stations [. . . ? . . .],[124]
114   amidst the rivers of understanding.
115   And you, O my elder, what have you undertaken?

[FERCHERTNE ANSWERED]

116   This is not difficult:
117   [to go] into the mountain of rank,[125]
118   into the communion of knowledge,
119   into the lands of men of understanding,
120   into the breast of poetic revision,
121   into the estuary of generosities,
122   at the assembly of the king's sire pig,[126]
123   in the little respect of new men,
124   on the slope of death, in that place where there is
      abundance of great honors.[127]
125   A question, O boy of teaching, what route did you
      take?

[NEDE ANSWERED]

126 This is not difficult:
127 on the white plain of knowledge,[128]
128 on the beard of a king,
129 on the forest of age,
130 on the back of the plow ox,[129]
131 on the clarity of the summer moon,[130]
132 on fine cheeses,[131]
133 on the dew of a goddess,[132]
134 by the rarity of wheat,
135 on a ford of fear,[133]
136 on the hips of a good dwelling.[134]
137 And you, O my elder, what route did you take?

[FERCHERTNE ANSWERED]

138 This is not difficult: on Lug's goad,[135]
139 on the breasts of gentle women,
140 on the foliage of a wood,
141 on the head of a spear,
142 on a silver tunic,
143 on a chariot frame without a bottom,[136]
144 on a bottom without frame,
145 on the three ignorances of the Son of the Young
      One.[137]
146 A question, O boy of teaching, whose son are you?

[NEDE ANSWERED]

147 This is not difficult:
148 [I am] the son of Poetry,
149 Poetry, daughter of Scrutiny,
150 Scrutiny, son of Meditation,
151 Meditation, daughter of Great Knowing,

152   Great Knowing, son of Seeking,

153   Seeking, daughter of Investigation,

154   Investigation, daughter of Great Knowing,

155   Great Knowing, son of Great Good Sense,

156   Great Good Sense, son of Comprehension,

157   Comprehension, daughter of Wisdom,

158   Wisdom, daughter of the three gods of Dana.[138]

159   And you, O my elder, whose son are you?

[FERCHERTNE ANSWERED]

160   This is not difficult:

161   I am the man who has been and who was not born,[139]

162   who was shrouded in his mother's breast,[140]

163   who was baptised after his death,[141]

164   who was tied to death from the moment he first appeared,[142]

165   [who is] the first spoken words of every living being,[143]

166   the crying out of every dead being,[144]

167   the A whose name is very high.[145]

168   A question, O boy of teaching, do you have any news?

[NEDE ANSWERED]

169   There is, in truth, good news,

170   bounteous sea [in fish],[146]

171   swarming coast,

172   the woods smile,

173   flight of leaves [?],[147]

174   the fruit trees prosper,[148]

175   growth of the wheat fields,

176   numerous swarms of bees,[149]

177   a radiant world,

178   a happy peace,

179   a lovely summer,

180 paid troops,
181 kings full of sun,
182 marvelous wisdom,
183 battles become remote,
184 everyone has his proper art,
185 worthy men,
186 sewing for women,
187 [. . . ? . . .],¹⁵⁰
188 treasures laugh,¹⁵¹
189 full merit [in war],
190 plenitude of every art,
191 all good men are handsome,
192 all news is good,
193 good news.
194 And you, O my elder, do you have any news?

[FERCHERTNE ANSWERED]

195 This is in truth terrible news: this will be an evil time
     that will last a long time, during which the chiefs will
     be numerous,
196 during which honors will be rare; the living will
     annihilate good judgment.¹⁵²
197 The world's livestock will be sterile.
198 Men will reject decency.
199 The defenders of the great lords will leave.
200 Men will be evil. [Good] kings will be rare. Usurpers
     will be numerous.
201 Disgraces will be legion. Every man will be disgraced.
202 Chariots will perish after the race.
203 Enemies will completely deplete the Plain of Niall.¹⁵³
204 Truth will no longer guarantee excellence.¹⁵⁴
205 The sentinels around the churches will be beaten.
206 All art will be buffoonery.

207   All lies will be chosen.

208   Each person will depart from his natural state

209   with pride and arrogance,

210   such that neither rank,

211   nor age,

212   nor honor,

213   nor dignity,

214   nor [poetic] art,

215   nor instruction will be respected.

216   Whosoever is intelligent will be broken.[155]

217   Every king will be poor.

218   All that is noble will be scorned,

219   all that is servile will be elevated,

220   such that neither god nor man will be worshiped.

221   The nobles will perish before usurpers through oppression by the men of the black spears.[156]

222   Faith will be destroyed.[157]

223   Sacrifices will be disturbed.[158]

224   The doorsteps of churches will be crumbled.[159]

225   The cells will be undermined.

226   Churches will be burned.

227   Kitchens will be devastated by avarice.[160]

228   Inhospitality will destroy the flowers.[161]

229   Fruit will fall by bad judgment.[162]

230   Everyone's path will be destroyed.

231   Dogs will inflict wounds to bodies such that each [. . . ? . . .] against his followers through blackness, rancor, and meanness.[163]

232   There will be a place of refuge for rancor and meanness at the end of the last world.

233   There will be numerous debates with the people of the arts.

234   Everyone will pay a satirist to satirize to his gain.

235 Everyone will impose limits on everyone else.

236 Betrayal will venture onto every hill, such that neither bed nor oath will be protected.

237 Everyone will harm his neighbor, such that every brother will betray the other.

238 Everyone will impress his friends with drink and food, such that there will be neither truth nor honor nor soul.

239 Misers will mutually harden one another's hearts.

240 Usurpers will satirize each other with torrents of blackness.

241 The grades will be reversed; the clergy will be forgotten; the sages will be scorned.

242 Music will degenerate into coarseness.

243 The warrior nature will degenerate into the nature of cells and clergy.

244 Wisdom will turn into false judgment.

245 The law of the lords will turn against the Church.

246 Evil will pass into the heads of croziers.

247 Every marriage will become adulterous.[164]

248 Immense pride and immense free-will will exist in the sons of peasants and good-for-nothings.

249 Immense avarice, immense inhospitality, and immense meanness will exist in the landholders, such that their [poetic] arts will be black.[165]

250 The great art of embroidery will pass over to the insane and the prostitutes, such that colorless clothing will come to be expected.

251 False judgment will pass into the house of kings and lords.

252 Ingratitude and cruelty will come into each mind, such that servants and servant girls will no longer serve their masters, such that king and lord will no

longer hear the requests of their districts, nor their judgments; such that stewards will no longer listen to the monks or to their people and such that they will no longer pay fees to the lord for what he is owed; such that the ecclesiastical beneficiary will no longer pay the dues owed to the church and the regular priest; such that wives will no longer accept the word of their husbands above them; such that sons and daughters will no longer serve their fathers and mothers; such that students will no longer rise in the presence of their teachers.

253   Everyone will turn his art into evil teaching and false intelligence in order to try to outdo his master, such that the youngest will find it good to be seated with his elder standing next to him; it will no longer be shameful for the king or the lord to go drinking and eating with the companion who serves him, or in the presence of his retinue or of the company who comes with him; it will no longer be shameful for a farmer to go eat after having closed his house to the man of art who has sold his honor and his soul for a coat and some food; everyone will turn against his companion in eating and drinking alone; envy will fill every man; the proud man will sell his honor and his soul for the price of a scruple.

254   Modesty will be rejected;

255   the people will be held up to ridicule;

256   the lords will be annihilated;

257   the ranks will be scorned;

258   Sunday will be dishonored.

259   Literature will be forgotten;[166]

260   poets will be annihilated.[167]

261   Truth will be abolished;

262   false judgment will appear in the usurpers of the last world;[168]

263   fruit will be burned after it appears by a crowd of strangers and good-for-nothings.

264   There will be too large crowds [of men] in all lands.

265   All lands will extend into the mountains.

266   Every forest will be a great plain. Every plain will be a great forest.

267   Everyone will become a slave along with his whole family.

268   After that will come numerous and cruel maladies,

269   sudden and frightening storms,

270   lightening with the shattering of trees.

271   Winter will have leaves;

272   summer will be dark;

273   autumn will be without harvest,

274   spring will be without flowers.

275   There will be death with famine.

276   [There will be] maladies on the hordes:[169]

277   vertigo, consumption, dropsy [. . . ? . . .], plague, swelling, fever.

278   Objects found which have no benefit, caches without treasures, many goods without men.[170]

279   Extinction of champions,

280   a lack of wheat,

281   perjury,

282   judgments made in anger,

283   death lasting three days and three nights for two-thirds of all men,

284   a third of these evils on the creatures of the seas and the forests.

285   After that will come seven years of lamentation,

286   the flowers will perish,

287   in every house there will be lamentation,
288   strangers will ravage the plain of Ireland,
289   men will serve men.[171]
290   There will be a battle around Cnamchaill,[172]
291   beautiful stutterers will be killed,[173]
292   daughters will conceive for their fathers,[174]
293   battles will be surrendered around famous sites.
294   There will be desolation around the hilltops of the Isle of Meadows.[175]
295   The sea will invade all lands having residences of the Land of Promise.[176]
296   Ireland will be abandoned seven years before the Judgment.[177]
297   There will be a period of mourning after the massacres.
298   After that will come signs of the birth of the Antichrist,
299   monsters will be born in every district,[178]
300   the ponds will turn against the flowers,
301   horse droppings will be the color of gold,
302   water will taste like wine,
303   the mountains will become perfect lands,[179]
304   peat bogs will become fields of flowers,
305   beehives will be burned in the mountains,
306   ocean waves on the shore will be delayed from one day to the next.
307   After that will come seven dark years.
308   They will hide the sky's lights,
309   at the death of the world, they will enter into the presence of the Judgment.
310   This will be the Judgment, O son; big news, terrifying news, an evil time.
311   Ferchertne said: a question, do you know, O small [in

age], great [in knowledge], O son of Adne, who is above you?

[NEDE ANSWERED]

312 This is not difficult. I know my God the Creator.
313 I know my most wise prophet.
314 I know my hazel tree of poetry.
315 I know my strong God.
316 I know the great poet and seer Ferchertne.
317 The boy then kneeled before him. Then Nede threw to Ferchertne the poet's robe, which he took off, and he rose from the poet's seat, where he was, to throw himself at Ferchertne's feet.[180] And Ferchertne said:

[FERCHERTNE SAID]

318 Remain, O small [in age], O great poet of understanding, O son of Adne . . .[181]

[FERCHERTNE SAID]

319 May you be praised and glorified!
320 May you be celebrated and powerful in the opinion of man and God.
321 May you be a vessel for poetry.[182]
322 May you be the arm of a king.[183]
323 May you be a rock for doctors.[184]
324 May you be the glory of Emain.
325 May you be higher than all.

[NEDE SAID]

326 May you yourself be under the same title, a tree with a single trunk. It is at the same time manly and indestructible,
327 a vessel for poetry.

328 The expression of a new wisdom. It is the intelligence of perfect people, the father with the son, the son with the father.[185]

329 The three fathers in question when reading: the father of the age, the father according to the flesh, father with son, the father of teaching.

330 My fleshly father [guardian] remains no longer.

331 My father [guardian] of teaching is not present.

332 It is you who are my father according to age.

333 It is you whom I recognize as such. May you be yourself.[186]

[THE END. AMEN]

Notes on the Text

IN ALL THE NOTES pertaining to the glosses, references to the *Book of Leinster* are indicated according to the lines of the diplomatic edition of Best and O'Brien.

1. The title is contained only in the Rawlinson manuscript B.502. It is restored in the Whitley Stokes edition that appeared in *Revue Celtique* 26 (1905) as well as in the diplomatic edition of the *Book of Leinster* (Dublin: Dublin Institute for Advanced Studies, 1965). On this subject, see the introduction. But there exist enough copies of the text (thirteen in all) and the title is mentioned often enough in the glossaries to be considered standard or archaic or, at least, archaistic.

   The list of manuscripts is established thus by d'Arbois de Jubainville in his *Essai d'un catalogue de la littérature épique de l'Irelande:*
   - Around 1150, *Book of Leinster*, pp. 186–88;
   - twelfth century, Oxford Bodleian Library, Rawlinson B.502, folios 60–62b, under the title of *Immacalam in dá thúarad*, which is also found in *Cormac's Glossary*, under the word *coth;*
   - fourteenth century (?), Trinity College Dublin, H.2.16, cols. 554–69;

- fifteenth century, T.C.D., H.2.17, pp. 185–87, 192–94;
- fifteenth century, T.C.D., H.2.12, #8;
- sixteenth century, T.C.D., H.3.18, pp. 152–57, 543–55, 656–700;
- sixteenth century, British Museum, Egerton 88, folio 75 rècto, col. 2;
- sixteenth century, R.I.A., 23.Q.6 (Academy, 35.5), p. 53, fragment;
- sixteenth century, T.C.D., H.21.15, pp. 71–78;
- seventeenth century (?). A ms. of this document was found with Colgan, who died in 1668; see Gilbert in *Fourth Report of the Royal Commission on Historical Mss.*, 1874, p. 611, col. 2. The same Mr. Gilbert points to two mss. of this document with the Franciscans of Dublin; he gives them the classification mark IV, *Fourth Report,* p. 601, col. 1, and the classification mark XXIX, *Fourth Report,* p. 605, col. 1. I did not have the skill to find them;
- eighteenth century, British Museum, Egerton 113, p. 3, with a partial translation into English;
- 1821, R.I.A., 23.E.13 (Academy, 5.5).

Of all these copies, only the three oldest constitute original versions and should be taken into consideration. They were used by Whitley Stokes, in his "The Colloquy of the Two Sages," *Revue Celtique* 26 [hereafter *RC*], pp. 4–64. They are, respectively:

- *Book of Leinster,* folios 186–88 (abbreviation *LL*);
- Rawlinson B.502, folios 60a.2–62b.2 (Rawlinson);
- *Yellow Book of Lecan,* cols. 549–69 (*YBL*).

The following have become otherwise obsolete or useless:

- the two pages summarizing the *Colloquy* in O'Curry, *Lectures on the Manuscript Materials of Ancient Irish History* (Dublin, 1861), pp. 383—84 (the excerpt from the text cited at p. 616, Appendix no. 125, is limited to one line: *ciasu fili fili immali tugen*);
- Whitley Stokes's note in *Three Irish Glossaries* (London, 1862), p. liv, which treats only the variation of the title "*Immacallaim in dá Thuarad* cited at Coth p. 12 and at Tethru p. 41. According to Mr. O'Curry, this was the same as the *Immacallaim in dá Suad*, which will be mentioned infra";
- a brief page by Heinrich Zimmer in the *Deutsche Literaturzeitung* of 1881, no. 8, p. 271;
- a short reference by Robert Atkinson, *The Book of Leinster*, contents, pp. 47–48.

Im(m)acallam is a reflexive pronominal compound of *im(m)* and *acallam*, which comes from the Old Irish *acaldam*, verbal noun of the deponent *ad-gládathar*, "he speaks." The word *acallam* by itself refers to the fact of speaking or addressing someone. The prefixed reflexive pronoun *im-* specifies the meaning of a "dialogue, talk, conversation" between two people (*Royal Irish Academy Dictionary*, A/1, 13). In the beginning, there is no nuance or lexical specialization of a philosophical or doctrinal discussion or debate. This remark being made, the most exact translation is probably "colloquy." Nevertheless, the general sense is fairly broad:

- "act of conversing," "mutual converse," "conversation," "colloquy";
- "debate" (in the negative sense);
- "sexual intercourse" (attested only once in the

Lebor Gabala, ed. Macalister, p. 26, § 26);
• "conference, council" (*R.I.A.D.*, I/2, 114).

Tuarad, "sage," is a word of multiple meanings that hardly appears except in this form and whose meaning in the title, "poet, sage," is a conjecture by Whitley Stokes (*RC* 16, p. 8 *ff*). Five main meanings are known under the simple form *tuar:*
• "sign," "omen," "portent";
• "foretelling," "foreboding," "prophesying";
• "act of meriting," "deserving," "winning," "gaining," "obtaining";
• "cultivation," "preparation," "tilling of land";
• "cultivated field," "tilled land" (*R.I.A.D.*, I/1, 340–41).

The simple form *tuar* is used in *Cormac's Glossary*, while the suffix *-a(id)* introduces a simple variant of the agent noun. The question is to know why this word is used when it would have been simpler to make it understood from the start that under consideration is a conversation of a "professional" nature between two druids. It could therefore just as well be translated as the "talk between two seers" or between two "prophets." To designate the two interlocutors, we would have rather expected *sui*, "sage," *file*, "poet," or better yet *drui*, "druid." It must be noted, however, independently of all other considerations, that the word *file* is, in Irish usage, much more frequent than *drui*. The reason for this is, not any kind of opposition between two "corporations," with, at the end, the triumph of one over the other, but Christianization, which made the written prevail over the oral; the *file* very naturally had, as a "seer," writing as one of his ordinary attributes (see *Les Druides*, pp. 263–70). As for the name for "sage," *sui*, it is perfectly synonymous with "druid," *drui*. There is even the example of the three *filid* of the king Conaire, who are named respectively Sui, Rosui, and Forsui, "Sage," "Great Sage" and "Very Great Sage" (*Togail Bruidne Da Derga*, "The Destruction of the Inn of Da Derga," *Lebor na hUidre* version, ed. Best and Bergin [Dublin, 1929], folio 94b, p. 234, line 7666; the text gives "Rodui" and "Fordui," which obviously needs to be corrected, as was done here).

2. The proper noun Adne (or Adnai) is understood as "old" by the Irish, who associate it with the adjective *sen*, "old," by a prefixed compound *ad-sena*, which is, strictly speaking, a glossary word. But it is probable that only the oldest mention of the name, by Cormac in the ninth century, is authentic and that the two other glossary writers, seven or eight centuries later, merely recopied. The word is considered as being "of doubtful status and meaning" by the *R.I.A.D.* (A/1, 63). The important thing here, however, is that the druid, because of his knowledge and experience, is almost automatically considered as old or leading an existence related to old age. We see, moreover, throughout the dialogue that what is going on here is a verbal joust between a young and an old poet with, as the final, inevitable result, the recognition by the young poet of the superiority of the old one.

3. *Túath*, plural *túatha*, is usually translated as *tribu* (English *tribe*). But this translation implies an erroneous semantic or "sociological" nuance. The meaning is at the same time geographical and human: *túath* simultaneously refers to the administrative subdivision

of the canton and of the people inhabiting it (see on this subject finally B. G. Scott's 'Tribes' and 'Tribalism' in Early Ireland," *Ogam*, 22–25 [1970–73], pp. 197–208). The expression *túatha nOlnecmacht* means that, at the beginning, Adne was the titled poet, not of one or of several cantons, but the most important poet of all of Connaught, and that, what is more, his grade was the highest of Ireland, which would tend to prove that the internal quarrels among the insular kingdoms had no influence on the conferring of druidic grades. All this obliges accepting the existence, not of an administrative hierarchy, but of a hierarchy of knowledge.

4. *Ól n-écmacht* is an ancient and archaic name for Connaught (*R.I.A.D.*, E, 42 and O, 139). For the explanation of this name, see my *Magie, médicine et divination chez les Celtes* (p. 113, n. 2.)

5. *Ollam* is the superlative of the adjective *oll*, "powerful." The word further serves as the equivalent and the translation of the English "doctor." It designates the highest grade of the druidic hierarchy. It is obvious, however, that such a hierarchy—in essence religious—is purely intellectual and not administrative (see on this subject Le Roux and Guyonvarc'h, *Les Druides*, 1986 ed., pp. 51–53). The "arch-druids" or "great druids," invented by contemporary neo-druidism in the nineteenth century, exist nowhere in the authentically Celtic nomenclatures. It can be seen in paragraph 6 that Nede, when he leaves from Scotland, holds the title of the elevated grade of *anruth*, which is the second of the whole hierarchy, but he is not yet *ollam* ("doctor") and he is, because of this fact, no match for Ferchertne.

6. The two words that we have rendered respectively as "science" and "poetry," *eicsi* and *filidecht,* are practically synonymous and designate, the one as well as the other, all the activities of a *file* or Irish poet in the domain of clairvoyance, divination, and wisdom. But whereas *filidecht* is an abstract substantive composed of the stem *filid* in the plural, plus a nominal suffix derived from *-echt,* (we have, on the same model, *druidecht,* "druidism," "druid science"), *eicsi* (modern *éigse*), while having the same meaning, is more recent (late Middle Irish and pre–Modern Irish) and is derived in all likelihood from a prefixed verb *do-écci,* "he sees" (*R.I.A.D.,* E, 75). The meaning of *druidecht* and *filidecht* deviated late toward magic, being attributed greatly and in bad part to the druids after Christianization. See my *Magie, médicine e divination chez les Celtes,* pp. 29–41 and p. 273.

7. As for the name Nede, there is no lexical or etymological reference to explain it, insofar as the meaning of the name could help in the explication of the character. Nede is fairly anciently known as the "bad" druid who, transgressing the obligations of his status, allows himself to be tempted by the wife of King Caier, his uncle, and satirizes the king in order to occupy the throne in his place and to possess at the same time sovereignty and queen. The story, which finishes very badly, is told *Cormac's Glossary,* in W. Stokes, *Three Irish Glossaries,* pp. xxxvi–xl). Cf. F Le Roux and C.-J. Guyonvarc'h, *Les Druides,* pp. 121–23 and, with more ample developments, *La Société celtique,* pp. 144–48; see also the analysis of magical technique in my *Magie, médicine et divination,* pp. 155–59.

8. Nede, Irish *file*, goes to Scotland to perfect his instruction and to receive druidic initiation, as the druids of Gaul, according to Caesar, went to Brittany to learn better their doctrine. The north and the islands in the north of the world are the obligatory destination of all the candidates for Celtic initiation, whatever the nature of the initiation, it being well understood that whoever is not worthy of it loses his reason when in contact with the higher truths. A question that has never been brought forward concerning these initiation voyages is that of language. If the Gallic and Irish druids went to receive or perfect their initiation in Scotland, there must have existed a common language understood by all the initiators and all the initiates. This obliges the postulation of a common Celtic language, a sacred language equivalent to Sanskrit and opposed to the "Prakrits" from which the neo-Celtic languages probably stem, as well as the few traces of Gallic discovered on the Continent. On all these questions, see Françoise Le Roux, "Les Îles au nord du monde," *Hommages à Albert Grenier* (Brussels: Latomus, 1961); vol. 2, pp. 1051–52, finally my article "Langue profane et langue sacrée," *Connaissance des religions*, 41–42 (June 1995), pp. 55–67, and my future works *Les Trois Initiations celtiques* and *Les Îles au nord du monde*. Furthermore, it should be noted that the regions in the north of Great Britain, otherwise known as the Highlands of Scotland, never had to submit to Roman occupation.

9. Eochu Echbel means "horse's mouth." This character is otherwise unknown. The Rawlinson manuscript ascribes, in its version, two other educators to Nede: "Co Gruibne n-ecess 7 co Crechduile 7 co Eochaid

nEchbel," "at Gruibne the poet's home, at Crechduile's home, and at Eochaid Echbel's home" (Whitley Stokes, *RC* 26, p. 8, n. 3). It is possible, if not
probable, that priestly initiation, exactly like warrior
initiation and, very likely, artisan initiation, was con-
ferred at the end of a teaching process dispensed by
several initiators, simultaneous or successive. In the
case of warrior initiation, however, it is the queen
warriors (Scathach and Aoife in Cúchulainn's case)
who dispense the teaching. Somewhat paradoxically,
it is on artisan initiation that we have the least information of medieval Irish origin.

10. The text literally says "an arrangement *[córus]* of
lamentation and moaning." The moaning of the wave
announcing a death is pointed out by Whitley Stokes
(*RC* 26, p. 9, n. 2) in a hagiographic text of the
Leabar Brécc, implicating Saint Columcille: *Atbert
Caindech: cid chanus in tond. Asbert Colum Cille: do
muntersa bói i ngabud anallana forsind fhairgi co epilt oen
dib,* "Said Caindech: what is the wave singing? Said
Columcille: thy household was in peril hitherto on
the sea, so that one of them perished." Here the saint,
by his gift of divination, is very much the successor of
the druid. An essential part of the magic attributed to
the druids by insular sources involves the mastery of
the elements: earth, water, air, fire, and fog (fifth element that corresponds to the Indians' *akasha*). See my
Magie, médicine, et divination chez les Celtes, pp.
166–77). The mastery of water goes together with
that of earth, wind, and fire, and it seems that it is
mentioned more frequently. This was noted in the
mythological text of *The Battle of Magh Tuireadh.*
When Lugh, before the battle, interrogates the

different specialists about what they will know to do in favor of the Túatha dé Dánann, the cup-bearing druid answers: "He said that he would carry away the twelve primary lakes of Ireland as witness that they [the Fomors] would find no water there, however much they might be seized with thirst. Here are which lakes they were: Derg-Loch, Loch Luimnigh, Loch nOrbsen, Loch Ri, Loch Mescdhae, Loch Cuan, Loch Laeig, Loch nEchach, Loch Fabail, Loch Deched, Loch Rioach. Marloch. They in turn would make their way to the twelve primary rivers of Ireland: Buas, Boann, Banna, Neim, Lai, Sinonn, Muaid, Sligech, Samair, Fionn, Riurtech, Siuir. They would all be hidden from the Fomors in such a way that they would find not a single drop of water in them. Drink, however, would be provided for the men of Ireland, even were they seven years in combat" (*Textes mythologiques irlandais*, vol.1, pp. 52–53, § 79). On the importance of water in Celtic religious concepts, see F. Le Roux and C.-J. Guyonvarc'h, *Les Druides*, pp. 315–22.

11. *Bricht* is a general term regarding the vocabulary of magic. It must be regretted that the text does not indicate the technical name of the incantation used and that it does not describe more fully the method used to cast the spell. The basic meaning of the word is "incantation," "charm," "magic spell" (*R.I.A.D.*, B, 187). The word is synonymous with *draoidheacht* (Middle Irish *druidecht*, "druidism"). But *bricht*, as to its generally accepted meaning, is closer to "charm," or "spell" than to "incantation," which assumes knowledge of very precise techniques, which are rarely described.

12. The reference to "after his death," which we would put in quotation marks, is particular to the Rawlinson B.502 manuscript. It adds nothing to the context. Power over water is one of the ordinary abilities of the *filid* (see note 10).

13. The use of the verb *ro gab,* "he seized," is identical to the use that describes the "taking" of royal power, that is, with the use of physical force. The substantive *ollamnas* "[dignity or office] of doctor" therefore indicates not only an "academic" grade but also an important and envied administrative position. It is of note, finally, that the robe of the *file* is the primary exterior indication of his position and that the word for it, *tuigen, tugan* (*R.I.A.D.*, T/2, 348) is reserved solely for it. The *file* Ferchertne is, moreover, a familiar face in the court of Ulster. He is frequently featured in the epic narratives, particularly in *The Cattle Raid of Cooley* (see note 24), and the *Yellow Book of Lecan* attributes to him a genealogy that, limited as it is, proves his importance: "son of Glas, son of Ross, son of Rudraige" (W. Stokes, *RC* 26, p. 9, n. 3). The opposition and the rivalries between Ulster and Connaught, allied most often with the other kingdoms of Ireland against Ulster, are part of the usual mythical, political, and even ethnic landscape of medieval Ireland, with some continuations even in our own era. The most complete illustration of this is the narrative of *The Cattle Raid of Cooley.*

14. Medieval Irish has no word that translates the two conjoined notions of "professor" and "student" such as the current structures of teaching in almost all the countries of Europe—primary, secondary, and post-secondary—limit our conception of them. In the

medieval Irish notion, the teacher is an *aite*, "guardian," while the student is a *dalta*, "ward," which is an indication of an adoptive bond, both legal and affective, between the two parties. The teaching, which is personal, takes place in the druid's home, more by immersion than by pedagogy, according to traditional methods very close to those of the Brahmans of India, with a small number of students who do not leave the master for a single instant. All this obviously has nothing in common with the "en masse" teaching at contemporary universities.

15. The master does not answer the question asked but he concludes in all likelihood that, because his student was able, through his spell, to know or understand what the sound of the wave meant, he has nothing left to teach him. There follows the formula for immediate dismissal, scarcely masked by his final praises. This is also implicit verification that the druid teaches in solitude without any collaboration with his colleagues whatsoever.

16. Eochaid recognizes the merit of the student: he has the knowledge of a doctor. But he does not confer upon him the grade, a detail that has importance for what follows in the narrative, either because he does not wish to do so, or more simply because his own grade does not permit him to do so. The word *eolas* refers to "understanding," especially that which is acquired through experience or an apprenticeship (I would readily say of the traditional type), as opposed to "knowledge" of the "academic" type, of which medieval Ireland had absolutely no idea (see the *R.I.A.D.*, E, 152–53). This text is, to my knowledge, the only one wherein it is clearly stated that two *filid*

who have reached the same level of understanding cannot live together.

17. The three brothers are mentioned only in this passage. The first two, Lugaid and Cairbre, have relatively common names. Only the last one named, Cruttine, has an unusual and, so to speak, predestined name: "little harp." Though it does not have the rigor of the Indians as to the separation of social classes, Ireland prefers and appreciates familial continuity in the practice of a profession or in the maintaining of an immutable social status. The narratives teem with families said to be royal, druidic, or artisan. There is no taboo nor any absolute legal obligation, but the preference is always expressed. This being the case, a druid can be the son of a warrior or an artisan and a king or a warrior can be the son of a druid. Examples abound in all the narratives.

18. With seeming naïveté, this paragraph describes fairly well the ideal and the requirements of the perfection of knowledge and understanding that are those of the traditional Irish scholars. The druid does not have the right to be ignorant of the least detail—such as the name for the reed or the stem of sanicle or the digitalis in any circumstance. The druid's privileged interlocutor—that is, the king—could, in effect, at any moment ask him any question whatsoever. And the druid was required, on pain of losing his position through untruth or ignorance (the two go hand in hand!), to produce the appropriate response. This explains in particular why the *filid* were so curious and so passionate about etymologies and genealogies. A further question can be asked as to why two of the three plants in question are medicinal plants.

Digitalis is well known in this regard. Sanicle, which is less so, is an umbellifer used in olden days for dysentery and spitting of blood (see Littré, *Dictionnaire de la langue française* [1873 ed.], vol. 4, p. 1821c). None of these three plants is referenced in the two lists of medicinal plants published by Whitley Stokes, "On the Materia Medica of the Mediaeval Irish, *Revue Celtique* 9 (1888), pp. 224–44).

19. Ireland is a relatively small country, and the detailed information about the itinerary of a trip is a constant device in all the narratives, be they epic, mythological, or simply annalistic or didactic (one may see, for example, the itinerary followed by the troops of Queen Medb at the time of their departure for the expedition against Ulster in the narrative of *The Cattle Raid of Cooley*). The place-names are sometimes mythical and cannot be found on any map of modern Ireland. More often they are still verifiable and easily identifiable.

20. The metal, gold, silver, or bronze branch is the insignia of the dignity of its possessor. This branch, as an insignia of dignity, is perhaps different from the magic "wand" that was used for incantations and magic procedures because, in this use, the wand is of mountain ash or hazel wood, but even when made of metal, the rod serves as protection against roving forces that could pose a threat to the *file* (in this sense, the *file*'s sword is a substitute for the wand and also has magic value or effectiveness). It should be noted that if the rod that is distinctive of dignity and grade is "above" the boy, in all likelihood it is not he who carries it but a servant in his escort (Nede had the right, because of his grade of *anruth*, to a suite of

twelve people). The rod could serve, above all, again magically, as protection for the crown *cakra.* The *anruth* comes in dignity immediately after the *ollam,* or "doctor" (superlative of *oll*, "powerful"). This is not about a grade analogous to those of our contemporary universities but about a degree of understanding and initiation. In any case, the word used here by the *Colloquy, craeb,* "branch," is different from what would have been expected, *flesc*, "rod," which does not have the initial magical connotation (see the *R.I.A.D.,* F/1, pp. 163–66).

21. Emain Macha, "capital" of Ulster, has been understood and interpreted as the "twins of Macha" through allusion to the story of the fairy Macha (another name for the Morrigan, or war goddess) whom Conchobar forbade to run against his horses while she was pregnant. She defeated the horses in the race and died, after having given birth to twins, a boy and a girl, and then having let out a cry that made all the Ulates weaker than a woman in labor for five days and four nights, or five nights and four days, for nine generations. See on this subject Françoise Le Roux and Christian-J. Guyonvarc'h, "Mórrigan-Bodb-Macha: La souveraineté guerrière d'Irlande," *Celticum* 25 (Rennes, 1983), pp. 29–68.

22. Bricriu, whose surname, Nemthenga, "of the poisoned tongue," describes him best, is an ambiguous character of Irish mythology, closely related in behavior to the Germanic Loki. Coming out again from the court of Ulster, he has no other ambition than to get the Ulates to fight among themselves. To this end, all lies are good, all is treachery and hypocrisy. One of the best condensed descriptions of this character is

Georges Dumézil's in *Loki* (1986 ed.), pp. 206–13. The appearance, though brief, of this mythological figure in *The Colloquy of Two Sages* suffices to place the narrative outside of all possible history and all real chronology. The narrative in which Bricriu is the principal actor is the *Fled Bricrend* (Bricriu's Feast); see G. Henderson, ed., *Irish Texts Society*, (London, 1899), vol. 2.

23. The *faitche*, or "open plain," or again "meadow," is the area of land, close to the royal residence but outside the ramparts or the fortification embankment, where the official assemblies and meetings were held, including the military exercises of the young people.

24. Ferchertne is the chief, or at least the most important of the *filid* of Ulster. In the great procession of the Ulates at the end of the narrative of the *The Cattle Raid of Cooley*," he is described thus:

> There came another troop toward this same hill of Slemain Mide, said Mac Roth. Well-honed and proud people, a royal troop with extraordinary garb, of white as well as blue, black, and purple, such that to a king are they comparable, all these well-honed and chosen men of this powerful and strange troop. It is food for the eye of many, to gaze upon their beauty and their appearance, as though this were, for each person of this troop, about going to an extraordinary, high feast. There are three distinguished men at the head of this troop. The first of them has a black cloak with gold-threaded edging, a brooch of gold on his cloak at his chest, a tunic of excellent silk next to his skin, sandals made of sheepskin. It is not often that there is among the

men of the world someone as handsome as he. He has hair light blond in color, a shining sword of ivory, with loops of golden thread in his right hand. He throws the ivory sword in the air such that it falls on the head of the man in the middle, whom the sword touches and touches not. He throws it again in the air, and it falls on the other man's head, the other man takes it in his hand and it harms neither of the two, if not for each one's head, and the two men do not see it. There are two young men with nice brown-colored skin and a brilliant appearance. They have a red and gray cloak, a brooch of white silver on their cloaks at their chests, a white-pommeled sword under their clothing, purple sandals. As harmonious as the strings of a harp between the hands of a sage when touched deliberately are the voice and the music of one of the men, such that hearing the sound of his voice is sufficient entertainment for the army. Worthy of a king or a candidate-king is each man of this troop as to clothing and demeanor. To look at them, you would think they were each and every one of them kings. They do not have spears or swords with them, but rather they are with their servants. "These are very proud people," says Ailill, "and who are they, O Fergus?" "I know," says Fergus. "They are the people of art, Ulates encircling Ferchertne, the rich white man at play whom you see, namely Ferchertne, the doctor of the Ulates. Before him the lakes and the rivers recede when he satirizes, and they swell in height when he praises them. The two others whom you saw, these are Athirne, the high poet, to whom men can refuse nothing, and Ailill of the honey tongue, son of Cerba, and he is called Ailill of the honey tongue because the words of science that come out of him are *sweet as honey*." (From Christian-J. Guyonvarc'h, *La Razzia des vaches de Cooley*, pp. 243–44; this and following passages from *La Razzia* translated from French by Clare Frock.)

Without Bricriu's intervention and lie, Nede would never have thought of occupying the chair left vacant by his father's death. He knew too well that Ferchertne was superior to him. But without this error, there would have been no dialogue.

25. The druid teaches compulsorily outside the agglomeration, preferably in a forest, which corresponds to the symbolism of his knowledge (which the wood naturally supports). The locale is identical in the case of the druid Cathbad according to the *Book of Leinster*'s version of *The Cattle Raid of Cooley:* "Cathbad the druid was giving the teaching to his students to the northeast of Emain, and eight students of the rank of druidic science were in his presence." C.-J. Guyonvarc'h, *La Razzia*, p. 92.

26. In an episode from *The Cattle Raid of Cooley*, Cúchulainn takes recourse in the same scheme so that a warrior from Connaught will agree to fight him. "Then Loch, son of Mofebais, was called into Ailill's and Medb's tent. 'What do you have for me?' said Loch. 'You must fight Cúchulainn,' said Medb. 'I will not go to this expedition, for it is neither honorable nor nice for me to approach a young and tender, beardless and hairless boy, especially as I have nothing to reproach him for [. . .]' Medb told her women to go and talk to

Cúchulainn to tell him to make himself a false beard. The women went to Cúchulainn and they told him to make himself a false beard: 'For it is not worthy of a fine warrior in the camp to go into combat against you while you are beardless.' So Cúchulainn put on a false beard, and he came onto the hill above the men of Ireland. He showed to all of them this beard." C.-J. Guyonvarc'h, *La Razzia*, p. 136.

27. The Celts have always had a predilection for gaily and vibrantly colored clothing. But this is the only description we have of the official robe of a high-ranking *file*. "White bronze" (*findruine*) is the Irish name for electrum. The color of the birds is not specified, but it could be, despite the imprecision of the text, that it concerned a robe of the feathers of an otherworldly bird, in other words the swan. And this detail could account for a part of the legend of Merlin in the Arthurian stories. The color of the robe would then be composed of two shades of white blended with the solar color of gold.

28. Bricriu's whole art consists of making each of his two successive interlocutors believe that they have legitimate rights to the position of doctor of Ireland. It is in fact this duplicity that provokes Nede's initial usurpation, then the quarrel and the debate between the two *filid*. But it is probable that an incident of this kind was fairly familiar to the Irish, though this is seldom affirmed in the transcriptions of the narratives.

29. There is a play on words with *dán* "art" (genitive *dána*), and secondarily "poetry," and Dána, genitive Dánann, the name of the great primordial feminine divinity of the Celts.

30. This paragraph transposes the debate between Nede

and Ferchertne into the political and military opposition of Connaught and Ulster under the mythological
reigns of the queen of Connaught, Medb, and of the
king of Ulster, Conchobar. This opposition is the
principal argument of the great epic narrative, to the
glory of the hero Cúchulainn, of *The Cattle Raid of
Cooley*. But seeking or attributing to all of this a historic date must be resisted. See my introduction to
the edition of this text (*La Razzia*, pp. 34–35). Here
ends the non-glossed part of the *Colloquy*, which can
be considered the introduction, establishing the set-
ting and the two characters. This fairly long introduction could have been added later in order to
present in a coherent manner the actual text. But the
state of the language is not any different.

31. *LL* gloss: "He would reveal himself after having sung
his poetic inspiration, that is, his wisdom" (*LL*
24261).

32. *LL* gloss: "This is how I can see that he is a son of
apprenticeship" (*LL* 24263). The affirmation does
not rest on a verification of Nede's knowledge but on
his physical aspect and on the observation that
follows.

33. *LL* gloss: "So he arranged for himself a beard with
grass" (*LL* 24265). The *file* is not fooled by the magic
scheme of the young man to appear older and thus
more serious.

34. *LL* gloss: "In the place where he was in the process of
reciting his wisdom" (*LL* 24267). In the Irish vocabulary there is no distinction between the sense of
"sing" and that of "recite," which indicates fairly well
how the *filid* recited their poems or, should the occasion arise, their incantations.

35. *LL* gloss: "Which sage of the poets is the poet who is Nede or the poet [. . . ? . . .]" (*LL* 24269).

36. *LL* gloss: "I have not heard of a debate over knowledge and I have not heard that there was something afoot with the son of Adne" (*LL* 24271–72).

37. *LL* gloss: "I have not heard it said that he has unfailing knowledge (*LL* 24274).

38. *LL* double gloss: "Pleasant is the seat in which Nede has seated himself, or by my letters, Nede is deceived by the seat in which he is seated, that is the seat of the position of doctor" (*LL* 24276–77). The meaning is that the seat of doctor is pleasant to occupy when one possesses the required titles, but that its occupation is disappointing and useless when the titles are absent, the absence of titles being, in the Irish medieval concept of qualifications, synonymous with inability.

39. The qualifier "honorable" *(onórda)* is enough to situate the debate in the mode of academic courtesy. Despite the liveliness of their opposition and the importance of the stakes, the two *filid* will not lapse into trading insults or invective. One senses already that the affair will finish as it must, with the younger man's recognition of the older man's superiority and with the blessing of the younger man by the older. It could not be otherwise in the Irish code of honor being paid to the oldest *filid*. Age is considered here as a sign of experience and wisdom.

40. *Sruith,* as an adjective, means "old," "senior," "venerable," and, as a substantive, "elder," "reverend person," "sage." The word occurs frequently in medieval Irish terminology and in the ecclesiastical literature, but it is possible that it formerly belonged to the specialized

vocabulary of the *filid* (*R.I.A.D.*, S, 370–80).

41. The elliptical compactness of the Irish phrase, literally "sage of teaching each sage," with the ellipsis of the verb, is found in all the Celtic languages in varying degrees and it is certainly the heir of a very distant past. *LL* gloss: "The teaching of each sage is pleasant" (*LL* 24282).

42. *LL* gloss: "That is, it is owed by the sage to be a reproach to all ignorant people" (*LL* 24282). The three vices that Ireland rejects in the same way as lying are ignorance in a druid, cowardliness in a warrior, and avarice in a king.

43. *LL* gloss: "That is, that because of this good prior vision, he wields his anger against us" (*LL* 24286).

44. The sense of "reproach" (*súg*, from the Latin *succus*, French *suc*) is not absolutely certain, but it is the only probable one. *LL* gloss: "That is, what kind of great [?] reproach you will have for me" (*LL* 24288).

45. *LL* gloss: "This pleases me, that you have hidden from me a pleasant route, O Ferchertne" (*LL* 24290).

46. *LL* gloss: "Slight or small is the failing of whoever is young unless the question pertains to his knowledge" (*LL* 24292–93).

47. *LL* gloss, which allows for clarification of the text: "Proceed, O noble, in a more legal manner" (*LL* 24295). Here Nede means that Ferchertne should not at all reproach him for ignorance as long as he has not given him his teaching. Lines 18 and 19 continue this response.

48. *LL* gloss: "This is a bad demonstration, this one now" (*LL* 24297).

49. *LL* gloss: "It is a bad test that you gave me a long time ago" (*LL* 24299).

50. *LL* gloss: "He gave me my share of life and treasures in my apprenticeship as a meager heir" (*LL* 24301).

51. *LL* gloss: "I have sucked the breast of a good man rich in treasures. He had the treasures of wisdom, that is, Eochu (*LL* 24303–4).

52. Exceptionally, this question is not glossed.

53. It seems that here the gloss has been joined to the text and that the gloss is both a commentary and a brief paraphrase of the text.

54. *LL* gloss: "That is, from the place where there is the meeting of wisdom" (*LL* 24309). Two words exist that differ only by the long stress: *gaíse*, "wisdom [?]" listed in the *R.I.A.D.*, G, 34, according to the *Saltair na Rann* 6027, and *gaise*, without the long stress, "an onrush," "a current," "a stream" according to the ms. D IV 2, 74rb28. *Gaíse* is dubiously associated by the *R.I.A.D.* with *gaeth*, "wind." One can glimpse an underlying metaphor with the "confluence of wisdom" likened or compared to the meeting of two or several rivers and with the wind being associated with the mind. The use of *gaíse* in our text is not listed by the *R.I.A.D.*

55. *LL* gloss: "That is, from the place where the perfection of goodness is found" (*LL* 24311).

56. *LL* gloss: "That is, from the place where there is harmony of poetry. Or else *trogan* is the name of the red color of the rising morning sun" (*LL* 24313–14). In fact, *trogan* is one of the names for autumn; see Christian-J. Guyonvarc'h and Françoise Le Roux, *Les Fêtes celtiques* (Rennes: Ouest-France, 1986), pp. 208–11.

57. *LL* gloss: "That is, the nine hazel trees of the Segais" (*LL* 24316); another gloss from the Rawlinson B 502 ms.: "The nine hazel trees of the Segais, here is what

their names are: Sall, Fall, Fufall, Finnam, Fonnam, Fofhudell, Cru, Crinnam, Cruanblae" (W. Stokes, *RC* 26, p. 18, n. 2). The source of the Sagais is a marvelous water that, because of its extreme purity, burned like fire. It is at this source, property of the god Nechtan (another name for Manannan), that his wife, Boand (eponym for the Boyne), came to purify herself after her adventure with the Dagda and the birth of her son Aoughus. But the water burned one of her eyes, one arm, and one leg, and followed her to the sea. (See Christian-J. Guyonvarc'h, "La Courtise d'Étain," Nechtan [NEPT-ONO] or the "fils de la soeur," *Celticum, Annexes étymologiques du commentaire de textes* 15 (1966), p. 377 ff. The hazel tree is a tree of science, and it is natural that the *filid* would claim themselves to refer it, claiming themselves to be an expression of the source from which they draw their inspiration.

58. *LL* gloss: "That is, poetic art, in other words, the poetry of inspiration and art of play. It is of hazel trees from which the sages' games are made that I came" (*LL* 24316–17).

59. *LL* gloss: "That is, in the manner of the order of men of poetry, in other words men of science" (*LL* 24321).

60. *LL* gloss: "That is, according to their understanding" (*LL* 24323).

61. *LL* gloss: "That is, by which the truth is judged" (*LL* 24323).

62. *LL* gloss: "That is, by which untruth increases toward the night" (*LL* 24326).

63. *LL* gloss: "That is, white when one praises, black when one satirizes, etc." (*LL* 24329).

64. *LL* gloss: "That is, through study" (*LL* 24331).

65. In *LL* 24331, the name Ferchertne and the locution *ni handsa* are on the same line. In the manuscript of the *Book of Leinster,* "Ferchertne" is in the margin (p. 818, n. 3).

66. *LL* gloss: "That is, according to the columns of the six ages of man" (*LL* 24334).

67. *LL* gloss: "That is, the Boyne, for she is in Leinster and she absorbed the river of knowledge" (*LL* 24336). Rivers and streams are supposed to participate in the poetic inspiration of the *filid* and, sometimes, in moments of anger, they oppose it. The treatise on the rights and duties of the poets, mentioned at the end of the introduction, among others, tells how the *file* Athirne had an argument with the river Modarn, who, in revenge against him, laid to waste the counties of Tyrone and southern Donegal. A poet's incantation was required for the river to recede and abandon on its shores all the innumerable precious objects it had carried away. Another anecdote concerns Athirne, whose wife had asked for a salmon. The river had refused, and Athirne had made a satire. But having feared the river's anger, he rapidly recited a palinode of praise. The Modarn, satisfied, retreated and left on her banks a multitude of salmon. E. J. Gwynn, *Eriu* 13/1 (Dublin, 1940), pp. 13–14.

68. *LL* gloss: "That is, that this is the name of Boand, wife of Nechtan. After having drunk the drink of knowledge, it is to him that Boand went" (*LL* 24338–39). Regarding Boand, unique feminine divinity of the Irish pantheon and of whose many names this is one, see the narratives grouped under the title of "La Courtise d'Étain" in the *Textes mythologiques irlandais*, vol. 1, pp. 141–81.

69. *LL* gloss: "That is, along the strength of the poetic science of Nuada, that is, that Nuado Necht is the name of a poet from Leinster, and it is he who had Boand as his wife" (*LL* 24342). Nuado Necht is a mythical character different from the Nuada, who is the god-king of the Túatha dé Dánann in the narrative of the *Second Battle of Magh Tuireadh*; see the *Textes mythologiques irlandais*, vol. 1, pp. 25–104. Here the "forearm of the wife of Nuada" is a metaphor referring to the river Boyne. Necht, a shortened form of Nechtan, is a Celtic equivalent for the Latin Neptunus.

70. *LL* gloss: "That is, along a fine land in his solar inspiration, that is, in his poetic science" (*LL* 24344).

71. *LL* gloss: "That is, that he knows where the moon is during the day and where the sun is during the night, or it is after the night and it is in the day that he comes" (*LL* 24346–47). It could be deduced from this gloss that the druids of Ireland, and especially those of Gaul, had a vast understanding of astronomy, which alone explains the Coligny calendar, which also served as the foundation for their work in astrology, thanks to which they could predict or prophesy with exactitude. But it is also certain that druidic astrology was far more perfected than that with which our era contents itself. See F. Le Roux and C.-J. Guyonva-vc'h, *Les Druides*, p. 57, n. 24.

72. This expression indicates thus the beginning of all understanding. It is clarified by an *LL* gloss: "That is, along the umbilical cord that departs from me in the poetic inspiration of the young man, or else in the poetic inspiration that is, erudite, or along my umbilical cord, that is, *nomen alicuius partis paruae quae sit in ore infantis in utero matris, cuius nomen est srinci*."

73. *Forcital*, verbal noun of *for-cain*, "instructs," "teaches" (*R.I.A.D.*, F/2, 318–19), is formed etymologically upon the noun for "song." All druidic teaching must thus have been chanted or sung.

74. *LL* gloss: "In person" (*LL* 24355). On account of his age, Nede is, in effect, physically "small."

75. *LL* gloss: "That is, in understanding" (LL 24356). This is the opposite of the preceding gloss but in "intellectual" terms.

76. *LL* gloss: "That is to say that he is very firm in the face of constraint" (*LL* 24360).

77. Uncertain translation.

78. *LL* gloss: "That is, I am as passionate as fire, or [. . . ? . . .] departed toward you like fire" (*LL* 24362).

79. *LL* gloss: "That is, the fire of poetry, namely the word with redness" (*LL* 24364). These two last glosses compare the poetry of the *file* to a blazing fire.

80. *LL* gloss: "The powerful sound of the good science with me" (*LL* 24366).

81. *LL* gloss: "That is, I am a source with an abundance of understanding" (*LL* 24368). The comparison of the *file* to a source from which come all knowing and understanding is a frequent theme of Irish poems. All this is derived from the notion that the Irish poets drew their inspiration from the cauldron of poetry, in other words from the well of the Segais, as well as from the streams and the lakes. The short text entitled "The Cauldron of Poesy" was transcribed and published by Annie Power, *Anecdota from Irish Manuscripts* (Halle-Dublin, 1913), vol. 5, pp. 22–28; P. L. Henry, "The Caldron of Poesy," *Studia Celtica* 14–15 (1979–80), pp. 114–28; L. Brearnach, "The Cauldron of Poesy," *Eriu* 32 (1981), pp. 45–91; see also Thomas

F. O'Rahilly, *Early Irish History and Mythology* (Dublin, 1946), pp. 322–32, and Vernam Hull, "Varia Hibernica," *Zeitschrift für Celtische Philologie* 29 (1964), pp. 321–24. Spring water is also associated with science and truth; Heinrich Wagner, "Studies in the Origins of Early Celtic Traditions," *Eriu* 26 (1976), pp. 1–11, produces several parallel examples in the Mesopotamian traditions; see also Myles Dillon, "Celt and Hindu," *Vishveshvaranand Indological Journal* 1, no. 2, p. 203 *ff*.

82. *LL* gloss: "That is, that my art is a blade of poetry" (*LL* 24370).

83. *LL* gloss: "I am just in my art" (*LL* 24372).

84. *LL* gloss: "With bitterness like fire" (*LL* 243724).

85. *LL* gloss: "I am exact when explaining the meaning of a poem" (*LL* 24380).

86. *LL* gloss: "I condense science" (*LL* 24388).

87. *LL* gloss: "I preserve art" (*LL* 24390).

88. *LL* gloss: "This sea of science is abundant" (*LL* 24392). All these responses define a manner of teaching founded on explanations, questions, interrogations, and enquiries. One must, above all, guard against taking the word "poetry" in the contemporary sense. It is here closer to "science" and "knowledge."

89. *LL* gloss: "Reddening faces through satire," or else "making praises until the shame of refusing treasures to the poets comes" (*LL* 24396).

90. *LL* gloss: "That is, the edge of satire into the flesh of anyone who does not respond to my art" (*LL* 24399); W. Stokes (*RC* 26, p. 23, n. 2) attributes to *LL* the following gloss, which starts what is our line 72, which is line 24403 in the diplomatic edition of Best and O'Brien (*LL*, vol. 4, p. 820): "Having no shame what-

soever in presenting demands"; then he follows this gloss with a Rawlinson gloss: That is, "the edge of satire, like a point in flesh, for him who does not respond [to my poems]." But, as to the sense, it seems indeed that Whitley Stokes is right.

91. *LL* gloss: "That is, the purification of poems through praise" (*LL* 24401).

92. *LL* gloss: "That is, teaching poetry" (*LL* 24405). The two words used respectively in the text and in the gloss to indicate "poetry," *creth* and *ecsi,* are rigorously synonymous, though the first is more archaic.

93. *LL* gloss: "That is, the pursuit of poetry" (*LL* 24410).

94. *LL* gloss: "That is, the art of every man in order to learn for the sake of the teaching of every man" (*LL* 24411).

95. *LL* gloss: "That is, spreading an abundance of science for everyone" (*LL* 24413).

96. *LL* gloss: "That is, subtle, who leaves off speaking until there is no disapproval against it" (*LL* 22415). All these glosses emphasize the different aspects and modes of expression, as well as the consequences of "poetry," that is, of the science, knowledge, and understanding of the *file.*

97. *LL* gloss: "I am habitually in bed with a king" (*LL* 24417). This gloss simply means that the poet is used to sitting next to the king, on the same seat, in order to converse familiarly. The glossed text suggests that the talks take place in a small room, that is, in the presence of only a few people, another sign of the familiarity of the druid and the king, the former counseling the latter and the latter showering the former with presents and gifts.

98. *LL* gloss: "That is, the little poems or the great poems

for which cows are given to the sage" (*LL* 24419). It was common to pay in this way for the *filid*'s recitations, poetic or otherwise, at royal parties (see p. 28).

99. *LL* gloss: "Numerous meters, or the abundance of poetry, or the barrier of the voice of every man, or of the Isle of Fal" (*LL* 24421). Fal is another name for Ireland.

100. *LL* gloss: "That is, the teaching to the apprenticed poets" (*LL* 24423).

101. *LL* gloss: "That is, that this is a desire of the kings, these brilliant narratives that come from me" (*LL* 24425).

102. *LL* gloss: "That is, to go hunting in order to ask for treasures and food" (*LL* 24429). This is the evocation, with absolute frankness, of the material preoccupations of the *filid*. The greater their notoriety, the greater their chances of obtaining elevated fees. The kings had a duty to themselves not to be avaricious and most often revealed themselves to be very generous. It may be noted that Saint Patrick also behaves like a *file* when, night falling, he seeks shelter and food and curses those who refuse him these. See the example cited in my *Magie, médicine et divination chez les Celtes*, pp. 175–77.

103. *LL* gloss: "That is, that I pray for everyone to be at peace, namely that [I render] a judgment for everyone" (*LL* 24431).

104. This brief phrase means that the *file* must keep order in his entourage when he asks for hospitality somewhere. He must above all take into account the hierarchy and the rank of the people whom he has at his disposition. The corresponding gloss specifies that "food is given according to troop, according to

degree, according to nobility, and according to number" (*LL* 24433–38).

105. *LL* gloss: "That is, that, in terms of dignity, I am with the king and I am part of the armed forces" (*LL* 24440). This concerns the tribulations of the *file* who accompanies the king on his travels and, should the occasion arise, on his military campaigns.

106. *LL* gloss: "I blush at the same time as the king" (*LL* 24444). This gloss is akin to the significance of the gloss listed in note 97. The *file* stresses with weight and insistence his qualifications as the king's companion.

107. *LL* gloss: "That is, the words of inspiration which walk after the Boyne. I consume the nuts that the Boyne brings, that is, the nuts of inspiration" (*LL* 24446–47). Nuts, indistinct from hazel nuts in the mythical definition, are considered the fruits of science and knowledge, which explains the metaphor in lines 28–29.

108. Here is how *Cormac's Glossary* describes the incantation called *briamon smetraich:* "He rubs the man's earlobe between his two fingers, and the man on whom this procedure is performed dies. This is natural: just as the ear is found on the outside of the man, the man on whom this procedure is performed finds himself placed outside of humanity." W. Stokes, *Three Irish Glossaries,* p. 14; cf. F. Le Roux and C.-J. Guyonvarc'h, *Les Druides,* p. 182.

109. Athirne is this mythical druid of Ulster who specializes in vicious, cruel, or at the very least unwarranted satire. His "shield" is a metaphor alluding to the three procedures he habitually uses to put an end to the resistance or the refusal of his victims: "satire,

supreme malediction, whims." On Athirne, see F. Le Roux and C.-J. Guyonvarc'h, *Les Druides*, pp. 206–7. Ireland has made of him the prototype of the "evil" druid, whose whims are unjustified and unlimited.

110. *LL* gloss: "Noble is the share I possess due to the excellence of my good science, namely my position of doctor" (*LL* 24463).

111. *LL* gloss: "It is a river, this share of inspiration of the good science that I have" (*LL* 24465).

112. *LL* gloss: "This is according to the mind of whomever I praise" (*LL* 24468).

113. The text thus indicates the narratives recounting war exploits, which the *LL* gloss corroborates: "That is, the narratives of merit and reproach of everyone before words" (*LL* 24472).

114. *LL* gloss: "I praise poetry following the path of the law" (*LL* 24476). This means that the *filid* understand their art as being in accord with all the provisions of the legal texts and jurisprudence, a sign of the extreme importance (which is not always properly evaluated or even recognized) of the law in Celtic (and in general, Indo-European) society.

115. *LL* gloss: "That is, that what I have found is as brilliant as a pearl" (*LL* 24478). The *file* in this way praises his poetic production.

116. *LL* gloss: "People make treasures prosper for me" (*LL* 24480).

117. *LL* gloss: "After the (poetic) meters" (*LL* 24482). The *nath* is the poetic meter reserved for the *anruth*, or *file* of the second grade, which comes immediately after the *ollam*.

118. The last three expressions probably indicate the relation of the *filid* with the people of the Otherworld

throughout the fleeting of human time, time to which the druid, theoretically and practically, must remain indifferent.

119. The word "king" in the text is metaphorical since it means both "king" and "wild boar" (*triath*). It is in the gloss that the common word *rí* is used: "following a king into his chambers" (*LL* 24492). Whitley Stokes surmises that this king is death, but I do not see the usefulness of such a supposition. The relation between the druid and king is a constant of the prerogatives and activities of the Celtic priestly class. See note 126.

120. This line is tied, in meaning, to the preceding one, though the exact meaning is not very clear: can the "dwelling made of clay" be the king's? The gloss confirms: "in a clay dwelling; in a clay and stone dwelling, that is to say a house made of clay and stone" (*LL* 24494–95). Celtic buildings, in Ireland as well as in Gaul and in insular Brittany, were made of wood, and a stone building was certainly exceptional. Also, the writing is awkward and repetitive.

121. The "head" of the candle must be the flame of the lit candle. Whitley Stokes (*RC* 26, p. 27), moreover, has understood it literally: "between candle and fire," which clearly is not in the text. But the gloss is even more enigmatic: "between burial and judgment" (*LL* 24497).

122. *LL* gloss: "That is, making peace between people in battle, and *that* is the horror of armed combat; or else between tree and house; that is, the paths between room and bed" (*LL* 24499–501). It seems that what is touched upon here is the capacity of the druids to make peace between two armies ready to battle each

other, but the end of the gloss is not clear. In Gaul, this capacity is attributed to the bards by Diodorus Siculus (*Histories,* 5.31.5): "Not only in the necessities of peace but further and especially in war, trust is placed in these philosophers and singing poets, and this with friends as well as enemies. Often on the battlefield, at the moment when armies are approaching one another, swords unsheathed, spears drawn, these bards come forward into the middle of the adversaries and calm them, as is done with wild animals using magic spells." Cf. Strabo, *Geography* 4.4; see F. Le Roux and C.-J. Guyonvarc'h, *Les Druides,* p. 15.

123. *LL* gloss: "That is, among the strong men of Tethra, that is, the name of a Fomorian king" (*LL* 24503). On the name Tethra, which is a borrowing of the Greek through the intermediary of Latin, see Françoise Le Roux and Christian-J. Guyonvarc'h, *La Souveraineté guerrière de l'Irlande* (Rennes: OGAM-Tradition celtique, 1983), pp. 125–32.

124. The end of the line contains an unexplained word.

125. The concern here is with the level and dignity of the grades of *filid,* the highest being of course that of *ollam,* or "doctor." The corresponding gloss states "in the nobility of the grade" (*LL* 24513).

126. There is a play on words coupled with a metaphor in the expression "a sire pig of the king [*torc treith*]." The explanation is in the *LL* gloss: "That is, at the assembly of the king's son, namely feather, feather bed, etc." (*LL* 24523). But *tríath,* "king," also contains the sense of "pig." The translation "of the sire pig [or wild boar]" must also not be rejected. This translation would be, then, an extreme metaphor in contradiction with the traditional idea, Celtic as well as Indo-

European, that makes the wild boar a priestly symbol. The wild boar is in fact never a royal symbol. The corresponding Welsh expression *twrch trwyth,* in the tale of Culhwch and Olwen, is a good example in pointing to a mythical wild boar.

127. The meaning of the words is clear, but the expression remains enigmatic.

128. The word used for "plain" also means "plank" or "board." This is perhaps an allusion to the wooden frame of a harp.

129. The expression is explained by a Rawlinson gloss: "my vigorous art" *(mo dán trén).* W. Stokes, *RC* 26, p. 29, n. 2. The metaphor is obscure.

130. *LL* gloss: "My art is vigorous as the light of a summer day, that is to say that when Sunday is nice, it frequently happens that Monday is nice in turn" (*LL* 24540–41). It seems that there was, in the *Book of Leinster,* the carrying over of a gloss from one line to another, perhaps because the deeper meaning, of the text as well as of the gloss, in the end escaped the most recent transcribers.

131. *LL* gloss: "On fine cheeses, namely acorns and fruit; or else the seven [poetic] meters" (*LL* 24543). If I understand this correctly, poetry is compared to a mode of progression of knowledge, and it is at the same time the *file*'s (spiritual?) nourishment. We know in any case that acorns are a "druidic" food. See below, note 161.

132. *LL* gloss: "Namely, wheat or else all kinds of teaching" (*LL* 24545). Whitley Stokes (*RC* 26, p. 29, n. 5) lists a more complete gloss from the manuscript H.3.18: "wheat and milk, that is, all kinds of teaching." He translates line 133 as "on dews of a goddess (corn and

milk)." The metaphor continues the preceding one.

133. *LL* gloss: "On the edge of the ford, fear is with everyone, that is, poetry" (*LL* 24550). This probably relates to making it understood that the *file*'s poetry (or science) is formidable and constitutes sufficient cause for fear.

134. *LL* gloss: "That is, the hips on another before the king of the dwelling which is in the house in the middle" (*LL* 24552). The "house in the middle" *(tech mid-chuarta)* is the royal residence of Tara, and the normal ambition of a *file* of high rank is to be received there, but the beginning of the text and of the corresponding gloss is not clear.

135. *LL* gloss: "It is Lugh who invented an assembly, a ball (of a slingshot) and a goad for horses" (*LL* 24556). The Celts did not use the whip for driving horses but the goad; on this subject, see Françoise Le Roux and Christian-J. Guyonvarc'h, *La civilisation celtique* (Rennes: Ouest-France, 1990; p. 27) and Christian-J. Guyonvarc'h, *The Cattle Raid of Cooley*, p. 77 and p. 303, n. 42. See also above, pp. 34–36. The reference to Lugh, supreme god of the Irish pantheon, is alone a guarantee of the authenticity of the ancientness of *The Colloquy of Two Sages*, especially in regard to such an archaic material detail. The term, furthermore, is not limited to Irish: *brot*, "goad," is found in the Breton *broud*, which has exactly the same meaning. In all likelihood, in question here is an ancient, divine, perhaps multifunctional "talisman." The other two references are of a mythological nature: the invention of the assembly *(oenach)* relates to the festival of Lughnasad, created by the god Lugh in honor of his mother, Tailtiu (see our work on *Les Fêtes celtiques*,

pp. 113–64). As for the slingshot ball, this is the one which, in the narrative of the *Cath Maighe Tuireadh*, or "Battle of Magh Tuireadh," enables him to kill the Fomorian king Balor, who is his own grandfather; see the *Textes mythologiques irlandais*, vol. 1, p. 57, § 135.

136. *LL* gloss: "That is, horses without chariots, or the framework of art" (*LL* 24567). If the metaphor, and its opposite in the following line, refers to poetry, it means on the one hand that poetry needs no "bottom" to exist on its own, and on the other hand, that, being itself a "bottom," it only needs its own existence to justify itself.

137. The "Son of the Young One" (Mac ind Óc), or Anghus, is the son of the Dagda and the goddess Boand (the Boyne). *LL* gloss: "That is, that he did not know when he would die, what kind of death would carry him away, and on what lump of earth he would die" (*LL* 24571–72). The *LL* text itself is erroneous and was rightly corrected by Whitley Stokes. The manuscript has *fessa* ("understandings"), which should be *anfessa* ("mistakes," "errors"). Mythological references are not numerous in the *Colloquy*, but they are sufficiently frequent to leave no doubt as to its ancient origins. Regarding the lump of earth as a symbol of sovereignty, see François Delpech, "La motte de terre: Symbole juridique et légendes de fondation," *Ollodagos* (1995), pp. 249–92.

138. This genealogy is ultimately, once again and always, that of the poet, who identifies himself to his art; *LL* gloss: "The three gods of Dana, the three sons of Brigit the poetess, that is, Brian, Luchar, and Uar, the three sons of Bres, son of Eladan and Brigit the poetess, daughter of the great Dagda, king of Ireland, was their

mother; and one of his [Dagda's] names was Ruad Rofessa ["Red with the Perfect Science"]; and Cermait, Dermait, and Aed [were the names of his sons]" (*LL* 24601–4).

139. Rawlinson manuscript gloss (W. Stokes, *RC* 26, p. 33, n. 1): "for there was no birth to Adam, but his formation from the four elements." The name of Adam is a biblical borrowing, but its use here corresponds to the Celtic notion of primordial man, universal, ageless, and without origin other than a global one of humanity or of a human group defined and represented by the members of the priestly class. The first man, in Celtic genesis, is always a druid. The Celts must have also had the triple notion of the world—material, celestial, and intellectual—such as it still survives in the Renaissance in Henry Cornelius Agrippa. Cf. *Les Trois Livres de la philosophie occulte ou magie*, Jean Servier, ed. (Paris, 1992), 1.1.31.

140. The explanation is held in one word in the *LL* gloss: "That is, in the earth" (*LL* 24617). This refers of course to the earth of Ireland, and to it alone. Christianization ultimately penetrated only very slightly into the Celtic notion of the "earth mother," considered as a mother both nurturing and protective, and also as a daughter, sister, and wife of the gods. The ethnic point takes precedence here over the Christian or pre-Christian religious point.

141. *LL* gloss: "That is, in the passion of Christ" (*LL* 24619).

142. *LL* gloss: "That is, the first appearance in which he was, this is the death of sin" (*LL* 24621).

143. Primordial man, who is the first living being, is also the first to die, and the spoken word is the first mani-

festation of life. The Celtic notion is joined here to that of the primordial tradition. This explains why, in popular Breton belief, the Ankou is either the first or the last death of the year. See Anatole Le Braz, *La Légende de la mort chez les Bretons amoricains* (Marseille: Laffite Reprints, 1983), vol. 2, pp. 111–12.

144. The formulation is parallel to the preceding one. It must be recalled that crying out, in the whole insular Celtic domain, has both legal and magical importance.

145. *LL* gloss: "It is noble and lofty, is his name, that is Ailm, that is Adam" (*LL* 24626). This line and the following gloss are the logical conclusion, superficially Christianized, of Ferchertne's series of responses.

146. The whole passage from line 161 to line 185 enumerates all the "good" news relating to the state and development of Ireland. See pp. 34–36.

147. *LL* gloss: "The leaves come out with poison, that is, paganism" (*LL* 24637). This gloss is one of the rare references to poison in the Irish texts, and it is one of the only ones that attribute it to paganism. Whitley Stokes asks the question: "Were they divining rods? or planchettes?" (*RC* 26, p. 33, n. 11). In my opinion, the question is not useful because poison does not belong to traditional magic but to sorcery, which is very different. The word that we translate as "leaf" literally means "wooden sheets," and this refers back to divination techniques. See Whitley Stokes's note, "Adamnan's Second Vision," *Revue Celtique* 12 (1891), p. 440, n. 11; see also my *Magie, médicine et divination chez les Celtes,* pp. 220–21.

148. *LL* gloss: "Sacred hosts and body of Christ" (*LL*

24639). But according to the corresponding glosses from Rawlinson and from the *Yellow Book of Lecan*, interpreting *ablanna* as "sacred hosts" (*R.I.A.D.*, A/1, 11) would be an erroneous reading for *abla upla* "apple trees and apples" (W. Stokes, *RC* 26, p. 35, n. 1). Or else the erroneous reading is pure chance, and in this case it is part of the accidents of transcription that alter the transmission of traditional fundamental ideas, or else it constitutes an element of the awkward Christianization of the *Colloquy*.

149. Keeping bees was an important agricultural activity of medieval Ireland, which elaborated a whole legislative structure on this subject; see Thomas Charles-Edward and Fergus Kelly, *Bechretha: An Old Irish Law-Tract on Bee-Keeping* (Dublin: Dublin Institute for Advanced Studies, 1983), *passim*. "For stealing receptacles that contain flies, the guilty person owes double the value of the receptacle or the price of the owner's honor" (d'Arbois de Jubainville, *Études sur le droit celtique*, vol. 2, p. 152, § 45). Cf. line 305, "beehives will be burned in the mountains." Mead being an intoxicating and priestly drink compared to the beer reserved for the warriors, it is little likely that bees were ever linked to the third productive function. Their symbolism would be closer to the primary priestly function.

150. Two unintelligible words.

151. Rawlinson gloss: "Treasures will laugh to the poets because of their meters" (W. Stokes, *RC* 26, p. 35, n. 4). A normal and balanced society is one in which the poets (in the medieval Irish sense of the word!) are duly honored and compensated by gifts or elevated fees.

152. It is remarkable that, among the number of major

calamities that will mark the end of the times, the *Colloquy*, via Ferchertne's mouth, enumerates in order the multiplication of chiefs, that is, governing leaders (no one will know anymore whom it is appropriate to obey), the rarity of honors paid to just and honest people (with, as a corollary, the general spread of dishonesty in political men), and the annihilation of good judgment; that is, two essential points: on the one hand, the perversion of the notion of sovereignty, and on the other, the deviation of justice. The sterility of livestock (primary cause of the poverty Ireland would experience), natural catastrophes, physical or intellectual disgrace, maladies, all kinds of accidents are considered, in a general way, inescapable consequences of these two violations of the cosmic order. In other words, all this can be regarded as diverse forms of punishment for all the varieties or kinds of lies that humanity tolerates or practices and that the gods punish.

153. The "Plain of Niall" is another name for Ireland (*LL* gloss: "That is, Ireland"; *LL* 24698).

154. Rawlinson gloss: "His justice or his wealth will no longer be protection for anyone." The absence of truth, corollary of lying, is the supreme calamity of the Celtic world.

155. *LL* gloss: "That is, that there will be the seizing of his cattle by people without money" (*LL* 24720).

156. These men of the black spears are the Scandinavians according to a gloss from the *Yellow Book of Lecan* (W. Stokes, *RC* 26, p. 39, n. 1).

157. *LL* gloss: "That is, without worship of God" (*LL* 24733). The Irish name for "faith" is that which, from the time of the conversion, was used to designate

Christianity: *cretem*, literally "belief." The use is Christian, but the word belongs to the Celtic heritage of Indo-European origin; see Christian-J. Guyonvarc'h, "Notes d'étymologie et de lexicographie gauloise et celtiques" 23, 161. "Irish *cretem* 'faith,' Welsh *credu*, Cornish *cresy*, Breton *krediñ*, 'to believe'; Irish *crábud*, Welsh *crefydd*, 'faith, devotion'; Irish *cretar*, Welsh *creir*, Breton *kreir(ioù)*, 'relics,'" (*Ogam*, 22–25 (1970–73), pp. 241–56. We no longer find in the Irish lexical uses, except by comparative etymology, the old semantic distinction made by Caesar in *De bello gallico* (6.13–16), in regard to the Gallic religion, between *disciplina* (doctrine), *religiones* (religious practices), and *res divinae* (cult envisaged in its material aspect), in Irish, respectively, *cretem*, *crábud* (Welsh *crefydd*), and *cretar*.

158. The Celtic name for "sacrifice," which is used here in the plural (*adbarta*), and which in fact indicates an "oblation" (the name for bloody sacrifice has apparently not been preserved), became, after Christianization, that of the Eucharist. It is probable that the word is meant here in this last meaning despite the plural; see Christian-J. Guyonvarc'h, "Introduction étymologique à l'étude du sacrifice dans la religion celtique," *Ogam* 35–36 (1983–84); *Études indoeuropéennes*, vol. 1, pp. 59–80.

159. Rawlinson gloss: "There will be stepping under the floors of the churches to steal out of them" (W. Stokes, *RC* 26, p. 39, n. 2).

160. *LL* gloss: "Without any food in them" (*LL* 24740).

161. *LL* gloss: "Acorns and fruit" (*LL* 24743). The first word, *mess*, means both "acorns" and "fruit," but more particularly "acorns." The reference to acorns

unavoidably refers to druidism. The manduction of acorns is furthermore linked to divination; see J. Zwicker, *Fontes Historiae Religionis Celticae* (Berlin, 1934), vol. 1, p. 51.

162. The traditional notion of natural calamity or catastrophe caused by human cruelty is particularly pronounced and perceivable in the Celtic tradition.

163. Rawlinson gloss: "Everyone will turn against the next to kill him" (W. Stokes, *RC* 26, p. 39, n. 6). The dog is normally, in the Celtic epic, an animal considered sympathetically, in contrast to what happens in the classical world and follows into Christianity. It is enough to think of the name of the great hero Cúchulainn ("Dog of Culann") and of the way in which it was given to him by a druid. See the narrative of the exploits of Cúchulainn's childhood in my *La Razzia des vaches de Cooley*, pp. 90–91. The basic idea of this line, taken up further in the following lines, is that the quintessence of evil will be reached when the priests themselves, and also the *filid*, will be contaminated by the surrounding cruelty of the end of the cycle. Such a notion is in itself very different from that of the Antichrist and of the Christian Apocalypse.

164. Marriage, in pre-Christian Ireland, is a legal and non-religious concept, and is concretized by a contract between two families rather than by the union of a man and a woman. It is Christianity that imposed the word *pósadh* (Old Irish *posaim*, from the Latin *sponsare* "commit oneself," "solemnly promise," then "marry"; J. Vendryes, *De hibernicis vocabulis quae a latina lingua originem duxerunt* [Paris: Klincksieck, 1902], pp. 167b–168a). The word passed into Irish from low, or dog, Latin through the intermediary of

Latin, which means that the borrowing was relatively late; J. Vendryes, *Lexique étymologiques de l'irlandais ancien* (Paris: Éditions du CNRS, 1960), p. 12. The *Colloquy* uses here the word *lanamnas*, "couple," which indicates a man and a woman living together, in the state of marriage generally, but not necessarily. Whitley Stokes (*RC* 26, p. 41, line 217) translates the word as "sexual connection," which is implicit but not explicit. The use of the word *adaltras*, "adulterer," however, borrowed from Latin, corresponds here to Christian morals of marriage.

165. Rawlinson gloss: "their songs and their stories and their eulogies" (W. Stokes, *RC* 26, p. 43, n. 2). There is a play on words between the word in the text *dána*, "arts," and the almost synonymous word in the gloss, *dúana*, "poems."

166. *Yellow Book of Lecan* gloss: "[there will come] a false meaning out of them" (W. Stokes, *RC* 26, p. 45, n. 1).

167. *LL* gloss: "That is, that there will no longer be any poets but only bards" (*LL* 24831). The bard lost his social position and was supplanted by the *filid*. On this question, see finally F. Le Roux and C.-J. Guyon-varc'h, *Les Druides* (1986 ed.), p. 33 *ff.*

168. Whitley Stokes (*RC* 26, p. 44) completed this with "by the usurpers," following the *Yellow Book of Lecan.*

169. The version in the *Book of Leinster* comes to an end at this line on account of a gap in the manuscript.

170. Rawlinson manuscript: "That is, many goods without men to consume them" (W. Stokes, *RC* 26, p. 47, n. 3). Under question are food as well as material riches.

171. Rawlinson gloss: "Every man will be attending another" (W. Stokes, *RC* 26, p. 47, n. 6). The text means that there will no longer exist any free men.

Following Irish jurisprudence, whoever is in financial dependence to another, either through debt or through contract of tenure, is in effect *doer*, not free.

172. Rawlinson gloss: "The rowing [rolling] wheel will proceed until it will be in contact with Cnámchaill" (W. Stokes, *RC* 26, p. 47, n. 7). The rolling wheel (*roth ramhach*) is obviously the cosmic wheel, without spokes or circumference, and which the mythical druid Mog Ruith ("Servant of the Wheel") both uses for his auguries and serves. This wheel has a particularity: "Blind will be whoever looks at it, deaf whoever hears it, dead whomever it falls upon"; see my *Magie, médicine et divination,* chapter 7, pp. 298–99. Cnámchaill is a toponym of which there exist several in Ireland; see Edmund Hogan, *Onomasticon Goidelicum* (Dublin, 1910), p. 272a.

173. By "stutterers" it must be understood here as people who do not understand Gaelic and speak a language disagreeable to the ears of the Irish of the Middle Ages, probably Scandinavians rather than Anglo-Saxons. They are perhaps "beautiful" because of their blond hair (likely conjecture by W. Stokes, *RC* 26, p. 47, n. 7: "The fair-haired Norsemen?").

174. Rawlinson gloss: "daughters will bear children to their fathers" (W. Stokes, *RC* 26, p. 47, n. 9). Incest has always horrified the Irish.

175. The Isle of Meadows is obviously Ireland.

176. Rawlinson gloss: "That is, when it will be near to inhabit the land which is promised to the saints" (W. Stokes, *RC* 26, p. 49, n. 2). Here there is assimilation of the Celtic Otherworld with the Paradise promised to the saints of Christianity.

177. The abandonment and destruction of Ireland by a

natural disaster (flood) seven years before the Judgment are parts of the funds of post-patrician Christian
predictions; see the *Tripartite Life*, pp. 117, 331, and
477. It is very possible, if not probable, that all this
goes back entirely or in part to the original Celtic
notion of the end of the world. This is not, in any
case, millenarianism. This links back as well to the
old Gallic belief, noted by Strabo (*Geography*, 4.4),
according to which, at the end of the times, "one day
fire and water alone will reign"; see F. Le Roux and
C.-J. Guyonvarc'h, *Les Druides*, p. 336.

178. Rawlinson gloss: "That is, two-headed ones" (W.
Stokes, *RC* 26, p. 49, n. 4). In all the medieval Irish
texts, deformity and physical anomaly (singleness of
eye, leg, and arm) are part of the signs or the marks of
the infernal world of the Fomors, who are the Celtic
equivalent of the Greek Titans and the Germanic
Vanirs. But this is the result of Christianization,
which relegated the Fomors to the infernal shadows.
Singleness of limb or organ is in fact the sign of the
primordiality of divine beings or of the Otherworld in
general.

179. The Otherworld is conceived as a flat land (cf. the
name of peninsular Brittany, Letavia, Breton Ledav,
Welsh Llydaw, Irish Letha, which is, in the Celtic
notion, both a flat land and the door to the Otherworld; see on this subject my *Magie, médicine et
divinization chez les Celtes*, pp. 315–16.

180. In one sense, the doctor's seat, occupied inappropriately
by a poet possessing neither the titles nor the knowledge
required, is comparable to the "seat perilous" of
Arthurian legend. But here there is no divine sanc-
tion because Nede, of his own accord, pays homage to

his master Ferchertne and leaves open the place that is owed to him. The importance accorded to the seat is, in principle, the same as in the narrative of the *Second Battle of Magh Tuireadh,* when Nuada remains standing for thirteen days in front of the god Lugh, seated on his own seat.

181. Rawlinson gloss: That is, "for the earth was swallowing him because of the discourtesy with which he treated the *ollave* in not rising up before him while the poet was standing" (W. Stokes, *RC* 26, p. 51, n. 2).

182. Rawlinson gloss: "Mayst thou be a keeper of poetry" (W. Stokes, *RC* 26, p. 51, n. 3).

183. Rawlinson gloss: "Mayst thou be at a king's hand" (W. Stokes, *RC* 26, p. 51, n. 4).

184. Rawlinson gloss: "Mayst thou be placed in ollaveship like an immoveable rock" (W. Stokes, *RC* 26, p. 53, n. 1).

185. One easily realizes, from reading these lines, the importance veiled by the questions of filiation and genealogy in the Celtic world. Here it obviously concerns only spiritual filiation, but this last counts at least as much as legal or natural filiation.

186. Nede proves his allegiance to Ferchertne and abandons all other spiritual filiation. The absence of the real father is not surprising since he is deceased. It is thus Ferchertne who will be from now on his titular guardian *(aite).* But according to Irish custom, we would have expected more consideration for the teaching instructor from Scotland.

Appendices

The Precepts of Cúchulainn

Seek not violent and vulgarly base quarrels,
be not proud, rude and haughty,
be not fearful, violent, impulsive, rash,
abase yourself not through wealth, which ruins
*   and intoxicates;*
be not the flea who spoils the beer in the king's
*   house,*
be not the man of lengthy sojourns on foreign
*   borders,*
seek not men without reputation or power,
miss not a deadline without legal justification;
recommend that one look to memory to determine
*   who is heir to the land,*
have the ancient historians justly and validly
*   interrogated in your presence;*
may there be found judges for the families and the
*   country,*
may the genealogies be extended when children are
*   born,*

may the living be summoned and, by their oaths,
*   may life be given back to the places where the*
*   deceased have lived,*
may heirs increase their goods according to natural
*   law,*
class foreigners according to the importance of
*   their rank.*
Argue not during lighthearted conversation,
speak not loudly,
play not the buffoon,
do not make use of mockery,
[. . . ? . . .] not the elders;
be ill-disposed toward no one,
ask for nothing difficult,
send no one away without according him his
*   request [?];*
agree gracefully, refuse gracefully, promise
*   gracefully;*
be humble before the teachings of the sages,
remember the rules established by the elders,
observe the ancestral laws;
have not a cold heart toward your friends,
be energetic against your enemies,
have not a querulous attitude in meetings,
be not overly talkative and insulting;
oppress not,
keep nothing that be not a benefit to you,
cover with your reprobation those who commit
*   injustices,*
condemn not the truth due to the desires of men,
break not contracts so as not to be repentant,

be not querulous so as not to be hateful,
be not lazy so as not to be weak,
be not overly hurried so as not to be vulgar.
Commit yourself to following these precepts, O
    my son.

The Grades of the Irish *Filid*

THE FOLLOWING IS A SUMMARY of etymological references to the names of the grades of Irish *filid* in my forthcoming *Prêtres et dieux des Celtes: Le vocabulaire sacerdotal du celtique* (Priests and Gods of the Celts: Celtic Priestly Vocabulary).

1. *Ollam*

Ollam is, morphologically, the superlative of the adjective *oll*, "great," "large," "vast" (*R.I.A.D.*, NOP, 136–37), and it is conceivable that, in common usage, the semantic ties with the base adjective have never been severed. But the substantivation is certainly very old since we can note the existence of two concurrent declined forms.

One has a consonantal ending, the genetive *olloman* (*LU* 302, 361), *ollomain* (*LU* 10306); the other is a palatized form, the genetive *ollaimh*, compared to *ollamhan* (*IGT* Dec § 52).

The two forms are used concurrently in the late Middle Irish texts, with no difference in use or meaning.

The basic definition is that found in *Cormac's Glossary:*

> *Ollamh .i. oll adhamh XXIIII. Ollamh .i. oll aúaim .i.*
> *amail is doiligh uaim bhís foaill do thoghail. Síc is doiligh*
> *saighidh for dhán 7 écsi inollamhan. Ollam din .i. oll éimh*
> *.i. oll di éimh .i. ollamh do éimh .i. émhid 7 ernes na cesta.[1]*

The text is the same with variations in detail in the *Yellow Book of Lecan:*

> *O) Ildam .i. oll a damh, an cethrar ar fichit. Aliter ollam .i.*
> *all-uaim .i. amail is doilig bis fo aill do t(h)ogail; nó saigid*
> *úaime bis fo aill, sic is doilig saigid for dan 7 écsi ind ollaman.*
> *Nó ollam .i. oll-diem .i. is oll immi dimess .i. cethrar ar*
> *fichit. Nó oll-dit-emid .i. ollam ernes na cesta.[2]*

The translation is from Codex A: "*Ollamh*, great is his suite: twenty-four [people]. *Ollam*, that is, *oll uaim*, 'large [is] his cave,' just as it is difficult to destroy a cave or a cliff *[sic]*, it is difficult to attack the art and poetry of a doctor; *ollam* also, is *oll eimh*, great at explaining, that is, that he explains and resolves questions."

Cormac's etymological games obviously have no scientific value. We must, however, examine them, or at least point them out, because the three suggested explanations are characteristic of the way in which medieval scholars conceived and explained the dignity and the knowledge of a *file* of the highest rank.

---

[1] Stokes, *Three Irish Glossaries*, p. 33, adapted from the Hodges and Smith manuscript 224, folios 3–67 of the Royal Irish Academy, which Stokes calls the Codex A; cf. Whitley Stokes, *Cormac's Glossary* (Calcutta, 1868), p. 127.

[2] Kuno Meyer, ed., *Anecdota from Irish Manuscripts* (Halle, 1913), vol. 5, pp. 85–86, § 998.

The first interpretation plays upon the Irish phonetic equivalence of the consonantal groups *il* and *id*. It suffices to introduce between *i* and *d* the possessive adjective *a*, "his," "her," to obtain *oll a damh*, "great [is] his troop." This observation only holds for the *Book of Lecan* version, but it is the oldest and is nowhere contradicted by Codex A.

The second interpretation, through *oll (a) uaim*, "great is his cave," is more subtle for the layman, in the sense that it places the dignity and the secret of the teaching in a cavern difficult to reach and to destroy. I absolutely do not believe that this is an invention or a whim of Cormac. It is better to think here of a fragment of traditional teaching that was no longer understood (on the symbolism of the cavern, see René Guénon, *Symboles de la science sacrée* [Paris: Gallimard, 1995]).

As to the third interpretation, it is almost superfluous to comment upon it because the intentions in it are so clear: the *ollam* is always the character in the best position to answer all questions and resolve problems, without distinction of nature or difficulty, that face his contemporaries.

O'Davoren's glossary, which comes much later, given that it was written at the beginning of 1569, is at the same time shorter and different:

"*Inloing .i. imfuilngi* ut est *inloing ollam anamain im fiulngither eolus anamna acon ollam,*" "*inloing,* that is, 'uphold,' *ut* is the *ollam* and upholds the poem *anamain,* the understanding of the *anamain* is upheld by the *ollam*" (Whitley Stokes, ed., *O'Davoren Glossary* [Halle: Archiv für Celtische Lexicographie, 1904], vol. 2, p. 385, #1072). The emphasis is placed here on the importance of poetic composition, successively in the active and in the passive.

But the picturesque, if the word is not too unusual in the circumstances, is in *O'Mulconry's Glossary*, again—and as always—edited by Whitley Stokes: "*an-Fili graece a filei amat dicitur .i. seircid foglamo. Nó fi. li .i. fí fora aeir 7 lí forae molad. Nó li ial .i. secht ngrad filed: ollam strut(h), cli, canae, dos, mac fuirmid, focluc.*" Translated, the text reads, "*Fili* in Greek from *filei* 'he loves' it is said, that is, lover of teaching. Or *fi-li*, that is *fi* because of satire and *li* because of praising. Or *li* 'generous,' that is, the seven grades of the *filid*: *ollam, ansruth, cli, canae, dos, mac fuirmid, focluc*" (*O'Mulconry's Glossary* [Halle: Archiv für Celtische Lexicographie, 1898], vol. 1, p. 260, § 537).

It could be that there are here again traces of traditional etymological play analogous to the Sanskrit *nirukta*. Such etymologies are common occurences in all medieval Irish erudition, which does not differ all that much from that of the rest of Europe of the same era. O'Mulconry is clearly inspired by the treatise of the *Crith Gablach*, a very long extract of which was published in *Les Druides* (1986 edition, pp. 50–52). It is obvious, nevertheless, that this brings us nothing positive as to the etymology and even less as to the meaning of the word.

There is, in any case, no distortion nor any break in meaning up to contemporary dictionaries. It will suffice to cite Patrick S. Dinnenn, *Foclóir Gaedhilge agus Bearla* (Dublin, 1927), p. 820b, who wisely enumerates the following meanings: "a master (of science or art), a chief poet, a professor, a doctor, a director, a learned man, a sage, a wizard." There is nothing further in Niall O'Dónaill's *Foclóir Gaeilge-Bearla* (Dublin, 1975), p. 930b, except, as a result of the orthographical simplifications in use since 1948, the suffixed derivative *ollamhanta*, now written as *ollúnta*, "professorial," and the substantive *ollamhnacht*, which became *ollúnacht*, "professorship."

In summary, to make this all well understood, modern

Irish *ollamh* is currently used, at the end of the semantic process, to translate the French academic title of "professor" and of "doctor," the one generally not going without the other in the same person, barring recent and unjustified exceptions.

Without much hesitation, we can make the few lines of the *R.I.A.D.* (NOP 138) that summarize the general state and status of the *ollam* our own:

> An ollave *was attached to the court of each of the provincial kings, often to those of subkings; and there seems (at some periods) to have been an* ard-ollam *who exercised authority over all the provincial* filidh. *The inferior grades of* "filidh" *had to discharge various offices for the ollave, such as keeping his two dogs (task of the* cana) *and fostering his children (that of the* drisech); *and the* erenaghs *(airchindig eclaisi) had to maintain his horses. Among his functions, according to the same passage, was that of guarding the king from occult dangers. (O'Curry, "Laws transcript,"* R.I.A.D., *239)*

It is hoped, for the dignity and efficacy of the *ollam*'s teaching, that the members of his suite sometimes had occupations other than those that are enumerated above. On the other hand, the last assertion is very likely true, though it is clearly expressed only here: *Dlegar don ollam beith i fail in rig im snamad die snadad ar siabrud*, "the *ollam* must be present at the king's side in Samain to protect him from demonic anger."

The etymology is without surprises according to J. Pokorny, whom we can follow without major worry. On the one hand, he notes that word is based on an Indo-European root *al, *ol, "darüber hinaus," the Old Irish *oll* serving to designate "anything, everything, that departs from the ordinary" (*Indogermanisches etymologisches Wörterbuch*, 24). On the other hand, closely connected to the Irish *oll* are the Welsh and Breton *holl*, the Cornish *oll*, "every," "all," the Latin *sollus*, "*totus* and *sobidus*," Tocharian A *salu*, "complete," B *sol-le*, "every," "all" (*IEW* 980).

Etymologically, the *ollam* is thus both the "all," or "everything," and the "extraordinary." By this definition, the word is akin to the primordiality of the first mythical druid, creator of the cult and instructor of the gods of Ireland. Nothing in effect authorizes the connection to a druidic sacerdotalism of the Gallic terms in *ollo*—listed by Holder (*Altceltischer Sprachschatz*, vol. 2, pp. 847–48)—even if there is an etymological relationship between these terms and the Irish *oll*. J. Vendryes (*Lexique étymologique de l'irlandais ancien*, 20–21) was already dubious, and D. Ellis Evans, *Gaulish Personal Names* (Oxford, 1967), pp. 237–38, is even more so, viz., "a hyper-Celticism for Germanic *al(l)a*—." When linguists have doubts, the truth is unknowable.

2. Anrad

The *anrad* (genitive singular *anrada*, nominative plural *anrai*) is the *file* or poet of second rank. The word is written in different ways: *anrud* (Cormac, YBL, 40); *anruth* (*Laws*, 4. 352.21); and *anradh* (*Irische Texte*, 3.5.9). The first meaning, which is also the most frequent, if not the most important, is the one we have indicated above, "poet" (*file*) of the second rank, inferior to the *ollam*, or "doctor."

The most important evidence is obviously *Cormac's Glossary*, which, in accordance with its usual practice, completes its definition with an analogical etymology. According to Whitley Stokes's Codex A, "*anruth* (.i. nomen gradus poet-

arum) sruth án (.i. nomen secundi gradus poetarum) cainmolta uad.i. sruth an inna la sruth namáne, chuige diiahessi" (*Three Irish Glossaries*, p. 3); and according to the *Yellow Book of Lecan*, *"anrud nomen secundi gradus poetarum .i. srut(h) án in cháinmolta úad ocus sruth ina mmóine chuige tar a n'écsi"* (Meyer, *Anecdota from Irish Manuscipts*, p. 4, § 40). The translation is simple: "*Ansruth, nomen secundi gradus poetarum*, that is, the rich current of the beautiful praise [which flows] from him, with the stream of treasures *-áne* [which flow] toward him in return" (*Cormac's Glossary*, p. 6).

It is little likely that the parenthetical Latin definition in Codex A is anything but a silent addition from Whitley Stokes. Otherwise, the only other thing to note is the analogical interpretation of *sruth*, "current" or "stream" (of science that flows from the *file* and of wealth that flows toward him in consequence of the gifts he receives).

But Cormac does not seem to know the second meaning of the word *anruth* confirmed in the legal texts, that is, a "name for a noble who is close to the king in dignity"; *"is é ansruth imid-ndich .i. ansruth a athir 7 a tsenathir 7 anruth fadesin, ar ni ansruth cert oinfer hi si(n),"* "it is an *ansruth* who protects [the king], whose father and grandfather are *ansruth*, for a typical *ansruth* is not a mere man" (R. Thurneysen, *Die Bürgschaft im irischen Recht*, p. 13, § 45).

Another only slighty different definition is in the commentary in the *Ancient Laws of Ireland*: *"ansruth .i. in fer imdith a mennut 7 a crich,"* that is, *"ansruth*, he is the man who defends his property and his territory, (*Laws*, vol. 4, pp. 348, 20; see *Bürgschaft*, p. 14). It cannot be concluded from this that there was a hereditary transmission of the grade, but it must be observed that Ireland valued the continuity of a noble, scholarly, and priestly tradition within the same family.

The third meaning depends on the second, "hero," "warrior," "champion," and it is confirmed this time in a few epic texts, by passages of the *eter erredaib 7 anrathaib* kind, "between heroes and warriors" (*LU* 10280). One of the best and clearest examples is found in the *Cattle Raid of Cooley*, *"ar ro fetammar is do maccaib anroth Ulad sut,"* "for we know that that man is one of the sons of the heroes of Ulster" (*Irische Texte*, vol. 5, p. 113, lines 909–10); German translation: *"denn wir wissen, jener ist von den Söhnen der Helden von Ulster,"* with, in note 3, reference to a passage from the *Togáil Troi*: *"Ba trom trá Iasón 7 la Hercoil 7 la ánrathu archena din sceoil sain,"* *"Iason und Herkules und die anderen Helden waren bedrückt in Folge dieser Botschaft"*; this sentence, however, is not found in the reference given, *Irische Texte*, vol. 2, p. 9, line 214. Still, it is surprising that J. Vendryes (*Lexique étymologique de l'irlandais ancien*, A–79), under the entry for *anrad*, has only retained the meaning of "champion," "warrior," following solely Windisch (in the *Wörterbuch*, vol. 1 of the *Irische Texte*, and the reference to the *TBC* given above), without indicating the fundamental meaning related to druidic sacerdotalism. The etymology provided does not seem reliable either: "It no doubt includes the adjective *án*, 'ardent,' 'noble,' followed by a word on which it is impossible to make a decision between several possible but not provable hypotheses." Besides *án*, genitive *áine*, "noble," "pure," "pleasant," "elegant," Dinneen (*Foclóir*, 1927 ed., p. 42a) lists only the *an-* that are grammatical or lexical tools. And I confess not knowing a single word in *-rád* or *-rud* that might suit, that is oriented toward the sense of "poet" or "warrior." *Anrud* is evidently not referenced in the *I.E.W.* of J. Pokorny, and if the *R.I.A.D.* (A 353–54) perfectly clarifies all semantic aspects, it provides no etymological leads.

3. *Clí*

The *R.I.A.D.* (C/2, 235–36) lists two substantives *clí*. The first has two meanings; either a "house-post," or, more figuratively, "champion," "support," "prop," "authority." The second, however, is the one that interests us: "the third highest in rank of the fili-grades," with semantic variants: "body" and "bosom," "heart."

In other words, without our having to enter too deeply here into the details of an abstruse bibliography, it is, first off, accepted fact that the case of *clí* is similar to that of *dos*; the name of the grade results from a metaphor. As sufficient proof, *Cormac's Glossary* will once again be cited:

> *Cli .i. a(r)achosmaile fri clii thige atrubrad .i. (is) besem inachad (no donclet) .is balc oc lár is coel oc clethe is direch inachad (no conclet) .is balc or lár is coel oc clethe is direch foeim doemar. dic clii iterna filedu. isbalc a suire inachrichiu fessin i(s) séim i crichu sectair. amail atcumaic in chlii insintégdais olár coclethi sic din atcumaic airechus ingraidse d(i)anad ainm clii inni bis isliu, dodemar com honní busuaisliu. is direch ambesaib adhana (oanruth cofoclachoin do eim dana cli inni bes islimdoemarson omní bes uaisli)*. . . .

> *Clí*. He was thus named due to his resemblance to a pillar. It is strong on the ground, it is thin at the top, and it shields and is shielded. Thus is the *clí* among the poets. He is strong in the inspection of his own territory, he is pleasant in outside territories. As is the pillar in the house from the ground to the top, so is the dignity of this grade, whence comes to him the name of *clí*. He shields what is under him, he is shielded by what is over him. He is straight in the practices of his poetry.[3]

[3]Codex A, pp. 10–11; *YBL*, *Anecdota from Irish Manuscripts*, p. 24 § 275; *Cormac's Glossary*, p. 34.

Now we have to come back to, or rather insist upon, the etymology and the duality of "poet/pillar" following an article by Calvert Watkins entitled *"Varia III. 1. Oir. clí and cleth "house-post"* (*Eriu* 29 [1978], pp. 155–61), which is in disagreement with the interpretations or rather the suggestions of the *R.I.A.D.* and those of J. Vendryes, *Lexique étymologique de l'irlandais ancien* (C–118).

It goes without saying, however, that the explanation given above is both philological and standard and that it takes into account Irish lexicographical and lexical customs. We are fully in *nirukta*, not to mention, by purely philological definition, analogical etymology. Let me simply add, before saying anything more about it, that, contrary to what often happens, all this remains perfectly coherent. But analogical etymology can mask true etymology. Calvert Watkins's study, in effect, emphasizes the existence of an ancient initial consonantal stem **klit-s* genitive **klit-os*, later dissociated into *clí* and *cleth*. The link must be made with the Sanskrit *srit-* "central post of the house," "support," the Homeric Greek κλίσιη, "well-built house," δικλίδες, "[door] having two jambs." All this is tied to the Indo-European stem **klei-*, "to prop or bear," "support," "incline" (*I.E.W.*, p. 601).

As an aside, it is fitting to make reference, finally, to a fourth *clí*, "apple tree," *clí .i. abull* according to the *Auraicept* 4282. It is doubtless a glossary word, and the *R.I.A.D.* (C/2, 237) is dubious. But it must not be forgotten that the apple is the fruit of knowledge and eternal youth. The link is easily made, symbolically or not, with the science of the *fili* and the quality of the "pillar" (of wood) of the *clí*.

4. Cana

There is relatively little to say about this word, though it designates a fairly highly elevated member of the hierarchy of *filid*. It has two principal meanings, "cub" or " whelp," or "poet of the fourth grade of *file*." Literally, the substantive *cana* (or *cano*) results from the evolution of a stem, *canont*, which is the agent noun of the well-known verbal stem *conaid*, "he sings." It is very possible, even probable, that the two confirmed meanings result from the confusing of two different words. This possibility is even stronger considering that Irish, like the other insular Celtic languages, lost the Indo-European name for wolf (*R.I.A.D.*, C/1, 65; R. Thurneysen, *Die Heldensage*, p. 69). What must be retained here is the semantic tie between poetic science and chanted song, which is its usual mode of expression.

5. Dos

The *dos* is the poet of the third year of studies and of the fifth rank of dignity. His particular song is the *laid*. He is compensated for each of his poems with a milk cow, and his suite is of four people (R. Thurneysen, *Mittelirische Verslehren*, in *Irische Texte*, vol. 3, pp. 114–16; *Ancient Laws of Ireland*, vol. 5, p. 26).

Cormac's Glossary offers, unusually, an interesting note devoted to the *dos*.

> "*Codex* A: Doss .i. ainm graid filead .i. arachosmaile fridoss as doss din in bliadain tanaise infochloc .i. cetheora duillne fair. cethrar dodhoss fortuaidh" (p. 15). *The* Yellow Book of Lecan has "Dos nomen gráidh fhiled .i. ar a chosmailius fri dos .i. dos didiu isin bliadain tánaisi in

fochlac .i. it *ceithreora duillne fair, cethar dano dám in dois
for túaith*" (in Kuno Meyer, *YBL*, p. 35, § 424).

The translation from Codex A reads, "*Doss*, that is, the
name of a grade of poet, in other words from his resemblance to a bush, that is, that the *dos* of the second year is
a *fochlac*, that is that he has four leaves on him, he has four
people with him in the territory" (*Cormac's Glossary*, p. 53).
The end of the passage from the *Yellow Book of Lecan* is
slightly different: "The *dos*'s suite is of four [people] in the
territory." The meaning of the metaphor, which is not very
clear at first reading, is that the *dos* is being compared to a
bush, and each of the four people in his retinue is compared
to a leaf of this bush.

But there exists a second entry for *dos* in the *Yellow Book
of Lecan* version: "*Doss .i. fili, quasi dírass .i. tinscra .i. tinde
argaid,*" "*Doss*, that is, poet, 'gift,' so to speak, that is compensation, namely silver ring" (Meyer, *YBL*, p. 39, § 459;
Stokes, *Cormac's Glossary*, p. 58). The meaning of the
metaphorical comparison rests on the notion of "compensation" tied to the monetary allowances of the poet. The
writer of the gloss includes it in the interpretation of his
name.

The name of the *dos* appears in the *Indogermanisches etymologisches Wörterbuch* of Pokorny (p. 178), but the meaning of "poet" is not mentioned. It treats only *doss*, "bush,"
related to the Latin *dumus* and to a whole group of Germanic words. But this closes the question. Contrary to the
indications in the dictionaries (the *Wörterbuch* by
Windisch, *Irische Texte*, vol. 1, p. 501a, and *R.I.A.D.*, D/2,
369), there are, therefore, not two words *dos(s)* in Irish, but
a single word *dos*, "bush," of which the name for the poet
is a metaphorical application. The *file* thus designated,

compared to the *filid* of high rank who would be "trees," is only a simple bush, due without question to the modesty of his understanding.

6. Mac fuirmid

With the *mac fuirmid*, poet in the second year of studies, starts the brief enumeration of the subordinate ranks. *Fuirmid* is the verbal noun of the verb *fo-ruimi* and the meaning of the substantive is apparently "a violent, aggressive effort," "blow," "thrust," etc. (*R.I.A.D.*, F/2, 482). We must therefore understand *mac fuirmid* literally as "the son of effort," which evokes the work of poetic training and, at the same time, scholarly restraint.

7. Fochlocon

The name of the *fochlocon*, sometimes written with the diminutive ending *-an*, *fochulán*, is also very often more simply written *fochloc*, which is in fact the name of an aquatic plant, perhaps cress (*R.I.A.D.*, F/2, 196–97). Despite his youth or inexperience (yet he had to know thirty narratives!), the *fochlocon* had the right to a particular meter, the *dian*, to a retinue of two people, and to a fee consisting of one heifer for one poem. The price for compensation due him in case of insult or injury varied according to whether or not he was the son of a *file*.

8. Taman

The word *taman* means first of all a "tree trunk" or a "rod"; then, through reference to the solidity of a trunk, a "chief" or "leader"; then, a "headless human body"; and finally, a "stupid man," a "hard head," or a "block of wood" (*R.I.A.D.*, T/1, 66). The metaphor extends therefore almost naturally to the beginner poet who does not yet know very much. An insane person was called *tamun* in the *Cattle Raid of Cooley*.

9. *Oblaire*

The name of the *oblaire* is linked by etymology to that of "apple," *uball* (*oball*) and to that of the "juggler" (who plays with apples). It is the last of the grades of *file*, and he apparently merited little esteem (he was required to know only seven narratives!). This is also the last of the three degrees of the *doerbáird*, or "unfree bards" (*R.I.A.D.*, NOP, 82; ZCP 14, p. 382, § 47).

Books of Related Interest

The Druids
CELTIC PRIESTS OF NATURE
by Jean Markale

Merlin
PRIEST OF NATURE
by Jean Markale

The Celts
UNCOVERING THE MYTHIC AND HISTORIC
ORIGINS OF WESTERN CULTURE
by Jean Markale

Women of the Celts
by Jean Markale

A Druid's Herbal for the Sacred Earth Year
by Ellen Evert Hopman

Being a Pagan
DRUIDS, WICCANS, AND WITCHES TODAY
by Ellen Evert Hopman

The Epics of Celtic Ireland
ANCIENT TALES OF MYSTERY AND MAGIC
by Jean Markale

The Pagan Mysteries of Halloween
CELEBRATING THE DARK HALF OF THE YEAR
by Jean Markale

Inner Traditions • Bear & Company
P.O. Box 388
Rochester, VT 05767
1-800-246-8648
www.InnerTraditions.com

Or contact your local bookseller